Pegg...

Love and Lemon Pie

Recipes for the Body and the Soul

Love and blessings,

Peggy Frezon

Acknowledgments

Many people have given their loving support in making this book a reality. Here are the names of just a few. My whole-hearted thanks go to:

Jesse Applewhite, Mary Boone, Ted Barnholdt, Mark Florian, Elaine Galloway, my son Justus Grose, Ken Harris, Glenda Rhyne, Faye Steger, Marcia Tompkins, and Etta Yvonne Wheeler, all of whom contributed some of their favorite recipes; Betty McMillan for proofreading, while Glenda, Faye and Mary helped test-cook for accuracy and clarity of some of my instructions.

My dear cousin, Beth Hunt-Erickson, former food writer for the *Minneapolis Star-Tribune* and author of *Wild Rice for All Seasons Cookbook*, who proofread the recipes and made suggestions for refinements. (Beth wrote under the name of Beth Anderson.) The book, still in print, has sold over 130,000 copies.

Cathy Munson, the artist, whose enthusiasm supported me and whose inspiration is evident in her art work.

Bob Lively, ordained minister, teacher-in-residence at Riverbend Church, and my own guru, who advised and supported me in this project.

Sammy Smith, my very special nephew and soulmate, (and a professional magician), who typeset the book and co-published the book the first printing.

The staff and volunteers at CASA, who embraced this project with enthusiasm.

My delightfully entertaining companion, my friend and devoted husband, Jim Kilpatrick, who was my support and main taste-tester.

Copyright © 2003 by Peggy S. Grose
First Edition, Third Printing, 2006

ISBN 0-9744213-1-6

Printed in China

Table of Contents

Acknowledgments – 2

Dedication – 8

A Letter from Home – 13

Appetizers And Snacks – 17
Bean Dip   17
Broccoli Dip   19
Cheese Straws   21
Chili Con Queso   23
Crab Dip   25
Cream Cheese Spread   25
Easy Fondue   27
Guacamole   27
Ken's Trash   29
Mexican Fondue   31
Nachos   33
Never Fail Microwave Peanut Brittle   35
Pickled Mushrooms   37
Toasted Pecans   37

Breads – 39
Banana Bread   39
Easy Holiday Pumpkin Bread   41
Foundation Sweet Dough   43
Ham and Corn Muffins   45
Hot Gingerbread   47
Hush Puppies   49

Lady Bird's Popovers   51
Refrigerator Bran Muffins   53
Smashed Biscuits   55
Spanish Cornbread   55
Zucchini Bread   57

Breakfasts – 59
Aunt Matsy's Foolproof Cheese Souffle   59
Breakfast Casserole   61
Cheese Bake   63
Cheese Grits   65
Cornmeal Waffles   67
Easy Poached Eggs   69
Egg Omelet   71
Eggs Benedict   73
French Toast with Orange Juice   73
Low-Cal Oatmeal   75
Mexican Breakfast   75
Microwave Low-Cal Oatmeal   77
Peasant Breakfast   79
Scrambled Eggs with Soda to Increase Volume   79
Southern Grits   81

Casseroles – 83
California Casserole   83
Chicken and Dressing Casserole   85
Chicken Cornbread Pie   87
Chili Casserole   89
Fiesta Lasagna   91
Ham and Hash Browns Casserole   93
King Ranch Casserole   95
Mary's Good-Enough-to-Be Junk-Food Casserole   97
Tamale Pie Casserole   99
Tuna Casserole   101
Turkey Manicotti   103

Desserts – 105
Beth's Lemon Chess Pie   105
Carrot Cake   107
Crumb Crust   109

Dark Sweet Cherries Parfait   109
Easy Pecan Pie   111
Egg Custard   113
Elaine's Lemon Icebox Pie   115
Heavenly Cake   117
Lemon Bars   119
Lemon Meringue Pie   121
Mama's Brownies   123
Mexican Chocolate Cake   125
Peach Crumb Cobbler   127
Pie Crust Made with Vegetable Shortening   129
Prune Whip   131
Strawberry Shortcake   133
Sweet Potato Pie   135

Main Dishes 137
Baked Ham   137
Beef Stew   139
Beef Stragonoff   141
Chicken and Rice   143
Chicken in a Slow-Cooker   145
Cranberry Chicken or Ham   145
Curried Beef   147
Curried Chicken and Rice   149
Faye's Pork Chops a l'Orange   151
Ginger Beef   153
Italian Meat Balls and Spaghetti Sauce   155
Jim's Easy Meat Loaf   157
Lemon Pork Chops   157
New England Baked Beans   159
Party Ham Balls in Brown Sauce   161
Sloppy Joes   161
Ted's Elegant Meat Loaf   163

Noodles, Potatoes, Rice 165
Baked Noodles   165
Baked Noodles Romanoff   167
Boiled Rice   167
Chinese Fried Rice   169

Fettucine Alfredo (Low Calorie)   171
Jesse's Spanish Rice   173
Macaroni and Cheese   175
Potatoes in Sour Cream   177
Rice Pilaf   177

Salads – 179
Cauliflower and Pasta Salad   179
Celery Stuffed with Cream Cheese   181
Chicken and Apple Salad   181
Cole Slaw   183
Cucumbers and Pineapple Salad   185
Egg Salad Sandwich Filling   185
Green Pea Salad   187
Pear and Cheese Salad   187
Rice, Bean and Corn Salad   189
Three Bean Salad   191
Tomato Aspic   193
Turkey Rice Salad   195

Sauces and Dressings – 197
Almond Sauce for Fish   197
Blender Hollandaise Sauce   199
Cooked Salad Dressing   201
Cranberry Sauce   203
Cucumber Sauce   203
Etta Yvonne's Apple Butter   205
Lemony Mayonnaise   207
Marinade for Beef   207
Mark's Grandmother's Barbecue Sauce   209
Orange Butter Syrup   209
Picante Sauce (Spicy Salsa)   211
Spiced Vinegar for Salads   211
Vinaigrette   213
White Sauce   213

Soups, Chowders and Stews – 215
Broccoli Soup   215
Chicken Chowder   217
Chicken Tortilla Soup   219

Corn Chowder   221
Cream of Onion Soup   223
Faye's Taco Soup   223
French Onion Soup   225
Glenda's Pizza Soup   225
Hearty Bean Soup   227
Mexican Vegetable Soup   229
Vegetable Soup   231

Vegetables – 233
Asparagus   233
Cabbage and Noodles   235
Corn Pudding   237
Creamed Onions   237
Easy Creamed Spinach   239
Garlic Green Beans   239
Glazed Carrots   241
Harvard Beets   241
Hopping John   243
Justus' Love Veggies   243
Sautéed Zucchini   245
Spinach Stuffing   245
Squash Elegante   247
Turnip Greens   247
Vegetable Stir-fry   249

About the Author – 250

To Order More Books – 251

𝒟edication

This book is dedicated to families and children every-where. Ten percent of the profits will be donated to CASA of Travis County, Inc., a nonprofit agency which provides trained guardians ad litem to represent children who have been removed from their homes because of abuse or neglect. These Court Appointed Special Advocates are each assigned one child or family of children, for whom they advocate from the time the children are removed from the home until a safe, permanent home is found. Sometimes, they maintain contact into adulthood.

CASA volunteers, appointed by the judge, spend hours researching and gathering information which they bring to the judge, with the ultimate goal of finding a safe, permanent home for each child. They spend time with the children, transporting them to appointments, listen-ing to their problems, and generally looking after their interests. They spend hours making phone calls to case-workers, attorneys, teachers, family members, foster parents, and therapists, in addition to appearing in court to deliver their reports to the judge. Occasionally they supervise parental visits.

There are over 42,000 CASA volunteers nationwide, with 710 CASA programs in all 50 states. A judge in Seattle, Washington, started the program in 1977 be-cause he needed more information about the children than he was getting in order to make the right decisions

for them. He envisioned well-trained citizens in the
community providing the court with a wealth of information and the child with a constant trusted friend. By 1982
the National Court Appointed Special Advocate Association was formed. It has been endorsed by the American
Bar Association, the National Council of Juvenile and
Family Court Judges, and the Office of Juvenile Justice
and Delinquency Prevention of the U. S. Department of
Justice. CASA of Travis County was formed in 1985 with
the help of a grant made by the Junior League of Austin.

Karen Cox, executive director of CASA, became involved out of an early experience of her own. She knew
what it was like to be a child in court with no advocate.
She declares, "I cannot tell you how devastating it is to be
a child, to speak, and have no one listen." When Karen
was 6, her mother died and she and her sister were left
with a mentally ill father. Thank goodness, their grand-
parents learned of the situation and, in a series of
dramatic events, rescued the girls.

Karen's CASA child, whom we will call "Mary," was in
a very abusive situation. The blue-eyed, blond girl, on
crutches with cerebral palsy, was first beaten with a 2 by
4 by her mother's boyfriend and later sexually abused by
him. When she was abused in the foster home where she
was placed, she asked to be returned home. "There, at
least, I know who to be afraid of and maybe I can protect
my brothers," she insisted. This story has a happy end-
ing. Mary needed surgery, which her mother had op-
posed, but, with the help of the Child Protective Services
(CPS) caseworker and CASA volunteer, she had the
surgery and was given a wheelchair. She was placed in
a second foster home and completed rehabilitation following the surgery.

Now, this child was not free for adoption and long-term
foster care wasn't the best solution. Karen and the
caseworker searched for any relatives, anywhere, who
might come to Mary's aid. Sure enough, the grandpar-
ents were located and they took her across the country

and into their home. Of course, Karen continued contact with Mary and, four years ago, attended her high school graduation. Mary later brought her boyfriend to meet Karen. The attorney who handled Mary's case commented, "We would never have come to this happy conclusion without the CASA worker."

Karen stresses the importance of having been given much authority by the courts and access to records and information. She says the judges depend greatly upon the CASA volunteers' information and opinions before making decisions that affect the children. They work closely with the CPS caseworkers, attorneys and therapists, as well as the judges. " It's in the best interest of the child if you go into the court as a team," she declares. She goes on to say that she looks upon CASA, not as a band-aid, but a means of getting to the source of the problem and that, "The difference that we make is astounding." She also avows that the CASA agency is a wonderful place to work. Her husband commented recently, "I've never seen you so happy."

Melissa Ferrell is another volunteer whose philosophy is, "To whom much is given, much is expected," and she appears to live out that belief. She confides that children are where her heart is and that CASA volunteers are the most wonderful people in the world. She stresses that the importance of CASA is that each volunteer works hands-on with one child or one sibling group, is consistent, and is there for the long haul. While she praises CPS caseworkers as dedicated and hardworking, she points out how shorthanded and overburdened they are.

Melissa currently works with young twin boys whose home background is horrifying, but she is seeing evidence that, with a lot of love and redirecting, they are making a turnaround. Melissa simply glows when she tells of how they squeal with delight when she calls them on the phone and how they are learning manners, appropriate behavior in the company of others, and how to function within structure and limits.

Melissa talks about her hollow victories as an attorney. "A win or loss for a large company is absorbed into the bottom line, but Timmy and Jimmy can't afford to lose. For them, the stakes are too high," she admits and goes on to say, "My life is enriched by every conversation I have with them."

As Melissa explains her ministry, she recalls the story about the starfish, which goes something like this: A huge number of starfish were grounded on the beach one day, when an individual saw them and began gathering as many as he could, tossing them back into the sea. Another person came along and protested, " What's the use? There are too many of them for you to make a difference." The rescuer responded, as he held up one little starfish, "True, but I can make a huge difference to this one." With so many abused and neglected children out there, think of the difference made in the lives of the children served.

Because there are not enough volunteers to match with each child in the legal system, CASAs are assigned to the most severe cases or the cases with the greatest need and fewest resources available. To serve all the children in need, CASA has to grow. Another factor adding to the urgency is a 1997 law mandating that a child achieve permanency within 12 months of the case entering the system. Thus the need to assign a CASA volunteer immediately to ensure that all crucial details involving the child are heard.

CASA volunteer Jeanene Smith observes that these children demonstrate grave concern for their siblings, all out of proportion to their ages—a heavy burden for ones so young and so needy themselves. She says she serves as mediator, guide, cheerleader, sounding board, and part-time mom.

Not all cases have happy endings and the one to which Jeanene is currently assigned is one of those. She can't promise these five kids that everything will be perfect, but she can assure them she'll stick with them. Her first goal is to get them to a safe place, then the work of nurturing, healing and growth can begin to take place.

Jeanene compares CASA volunteers with the Good Samaritan in the parable told by Jesus. The expression "good Samaritan" was an oxymoron—in people's minds, there was no such thing as a "good" Samaritan. And remember, two people, including a priest, passed the wounded traveler before the Samaritan stopped to help him. Likewise, many children served by CASA are passed by and left wounded on the proverbial side of the road. CASA volunteers get to do the highest calling by bandaging up the wounds of these small travelers, ensuring that they have shelter and food and providing what they so desperately need—a voice.

"Because we're in a volunteer situation," Jeanene explains, "We can ask questions that paid caseworkers are not permitted to ask. We can talk about personal matters, ask them how they like their childhood. We can pull strings, 'shake money out of the trees,' and otherwise get creative." She points out the support and respect that are given to CASA workers by the judges.

Jeanene admonishes everyone who doesn't know about CASA to find out. "Everyone can do something," she insists. "Be an advocate or just help in the office, stuffing envelopes, running errands, making phone calls. Or—just write a check."*

*CASA, 6330 Hwy. 290 East, Suite 350, Austin, Texas 78723, (512) 459-2272 / e-mail: casatc@aol.com / www.casatravis.org

A Letter from Home

Austin, Texas

Dear Reader,

Preparing, serving and eating food has great emotional meaning in most cultures, including our own. Holidays are feast days. The words "Thanksgiving" and "turkey" go together, creating a mental picture of ourselves around the table with family and friends. We feel warm and secure. When we are sick, we feel comforted by family and friends who bring chicken soup. The soup, as a symbol that someone cares, is just as important to our recovery as are the nutrients in it. A birthday calls for a cake that says this is our day—and ours alone. It would not seem special without that cake.

Preparing and serving food is one main way of showing we care. To put it in academic terms, we communicate nonverbally that we care, not realizing that nonverbal communication is easily missed or misinterpreted by the receiver. Our thoughts and feelings are best communicated when the verbal accompanies the nonverbal and when they are congruent—when the words match the action. The words help the receiver interpret the action accurately. We often spend enormous amounts of money and effort in preparing food because we love and care for someone, only to have the message completely bypass them because we failed to serve it up with loving words.

I learned to cook standing beside my mother, who gave completely of herself in her very successful efforts to please those who came to her table. Her reputation rested upon her scrumptious creations. We lived on the farm and, so, had plenty of fruits and vegetables, fresh from the garden, nuts from the orchard, beef, pork, chicken and eggs from the barnyard and, sometimes, wild game brought in by my father. My father and brothers worked hard and ate heartily. Occasionally we fed hired hands. Friends and relatives from the city came in hordes, especially in summer when there were plenty of fresh vegetables, peanuts, watermelons and canta-loupes. Being the only girl in the family, my place was usually beside my mother, helping her prepare meals and helping to freeze and can food for the coming winter.

Besides the procedures of cooking, I learned, from her example, that what it takes to be a good cook is a willingness to take the trouble to do it right. Like the greeting card slogan says, "When you care enough to send the very best."

When my four sons were still in elementary school, I began studying interpersonal communication and parenting. I learned that, if I served the family lunch with plenty of love and laughter, it didn't matter so much what I put on their plates. Or, even if I served up the very finest food, its importance would be lost if I failed to serve it with love.

This book is a guide for nurturing your relationships with those you love and care about, as well as a collection of recipes for nourishing their bodies.

I understand how busy you are and that probably you seldom have time to sit and read an entire book on inter-personal communication. So that is why I have arranged this book the way I have—so that you can read my suggestions while you stir the oatmeal or watch the lemon meringue pie.

I have been collecting recipes for 45 years. Some of the ones in this book are original with me, some are adaptations of those I have picked up while living in different parts of the world and many were given to me by others. As far as possible, I have not used recipes that were obviously from publications such as nationally distributed cookbooks or from our own local newspaper food column without considerable modifications. If I have used a previously-published recipe, this inclusion was wholly inadvertent. On another note, in order to avoid the awkwardness of the she/he, his/her usage in the text of this book, I have simply alternated the use of those male-female personal pronouns.

I believe it was God who gave me the idea for *Love And Lemon Pie*. It was several years ago that the whole thing came to me in one flash—the title, the front cover design, and the inside format. I hope that using this volume will be as great a blessing for you as writing it has been for me. I would be honored to hear from you with your stories, your responses to this book and your favorite recipes, if you wish. You may reach me through my email: peggy@loveandlemonpie.com. Also, see my website: *loveandlemonpie.com*.

Sincerely,

Peggy S. Grose

The quality of our relationships is directly
and totally determined by the quality of our
communication.

If our words consist of blame, criticism, and
sarcasm, our relationships will consist of fear,
defensiveness, and stagnation.

If our words consist of love, appreciation, and
encouragement, our relationships will consist of
trust, openness, and growth.

Appetizers and Snacks

Bean Dip

1 medium onion, chopped
1 (16-ounce) can vegetarian refried beans
1 ripe avocado
1 (1.25-ounce) package taco seasoning
1 cup sour cream (Fat-free works fine.)
1 cup shredded Cheddar cheese
1 cup tomatoes, chopped

In a 1-quart bowl, mix the onions with the refried beans. In a separate, small bowl, mash the avocado. Add the taco seasoning to the sour cream.

In a 13 x 9 x 2-inch dish, layer the ingredients as follows: beans, avocado, sour cream, cheese, and chopped tomatoes.

Serve with tortilla chips.

Serves 10-12.

Communication is a transaction, an exchange between two people—the speaker and the listener. Both are equally responsible for making the communication work.

If the speaker's words and the listener's inter-pretation of them don't match, we do not have effective communication. Check to make sure you "got it."

Broccoli Dip

1 cup onions, cut into 1-inch chunks
1 cup celery, cut into 1-inch chunks
1 (10-3/4-ounce) can cream of mushroom soup
1 (10-ounce) pkg. broccoli, cooked as directed
1 stick butter or margarine, softened
1-1/2 (6-ounce) sticks pasteurized process cheese
  with garlic, cut into cubes

Chop the onions, celery, and broccoli, with the mushroom soup, in the blender. Pour into a 1-1/2-quart chafing dish, heat, and stir in the butter and cheese.
Serve warm with crackers or chips.

*A*sking equals listening. Telling equals talking. Asking and listening are better than
telling and talking.

*When we do more talking than listening, we're
overdrawing from the bank.*

Cheese Straws

2 cups all-purpose flour
1 teaspoon baking powder
1/2 teaspoon salt
1/2 teaspoon cayenne pepper
1/2 teaspoon paprika
2 cups grated sharp Cheddar cheese
3/4 cup butter or margarine, softened
1/2 cup water
Topping:
Grated Parmesan cheese
Poppy or sesame seeds

Grease or line a 13 x 9 x 2-inch baking sheet with parchment paper. Combine the flour, baking powder, salt, cayenne pepper, paprika, cheese, and butter or margarine in a bowl and mix well. Add the water a little at a time to make a very stiff dough.

On a lightly floured surface, roll pieces of the dough into "sticks" slightly thicker than pencils. Cut the "sticks" into 4- or 5-inch lengths and flatten out. Arrange on the baking sheet. Sprinkle with the Parmesan cheese, poppy and/or sesame seeds.

Bake at 400° for about 10 minutes or until browned.

To make the straws crisper, reheat for 5 minutes just before serving.

Makes 4 dozen.

*H*ow to listen so they'll talk: Imagine how
much you'll gain by trying to "get" what the
other person is trying to say.

When we try to analyze another's problem,
thinking we can fix it, we're not listening.

Sometimes, listening is simply helping that
other person get through a difficult situation or
arrive at a solution.

Listen with a "third ear."

Chili Con Queso

1 (1-pound) can Italian-style tomatoes
  chopped in the blender for 3 seconds
1/2 teaspoon finely chopped garlic
1/2 teaspoon salt
1/2 teaspoon black pepper
1/4 to 1/2 teaspoon cayenne pepper,
  according to taste
1 (4-ounce) can chopped green chilies
2 tablespoons butter
2 tablespoons all-purpose flour
1 cup fat-free evaporated milk
3-1/2 cups shredded Monterey Jack cheese
Corn or tortilla chips

In a 2-1/2 quart saucepan, combine tomatoes, garlic, salt, black pepper, cayenne pepper, and chilies. Cook briskly, uncovered, until the mixture thickens. Set aside.

In a 1-quart saucepan, melt the butter over moderate heat. Add flour and mix well, stirring constantly.

Pour the evaporated milk into the butter-flour mixture in a slow stream and cook over moderate heat, stirring, until the sauce just begins to boil, thickens, and is smooth. Reduce heat to low and simmer 2-3 minutes.

Stir into the tomato mixture and return to the heat. Without letting the mixture boil, stir in the cheese, a handful at a time.

Serve with corn chips or tortilla chips.

Makes about 3-1/2 cups.

*E*ach person, deep down, knows the solutions
to her own problems. She just needs the
"space" to discover it.

When you listen, you are creating the "space"
the other person needs in order to discover the
solutions to her own problems.

Crab Dip

1/2 cup cilantro, washed and picked from stem
1 (8-ounce) carton soft cream cheese
1 bunch green onions, chopped
1/2 teaspoon Worcestershire sauce
3/4 cup cocktail sauce
3 or 4 dashes Louisiana hot sauce (not Tabasco)
Salt and pepper to taste
1 pound crab meat, chopped fine

Put the cilantro in the blender with enough water to cover and blend for 3 or 4 seconds. Drain thoroughly.

In a 1-quart bowl, mix the cream cheese, onions, and seasonings. Add crab meat and cilantro.

Serve with crackers or in a stuffed tomato.

Makes about 4 cups.

Cream Cheese Spread

1 (8-ounce) package regular cream cheese,
    softened
1/2 cup Mexican-style picante sauce (spicy salsa)
Dash fresh ground black pepper

Mix all ingredients.
Serve on crackers or chips.
Makes 1-1/2 cups spread.

*H*ow to listen so they'll talk: Resist the urge to scold, act shocked, or give advice. Put all judgment aside, at least for the moment. Being empathetic doesn't mean you approve, necessarily.

If you have trouble not talking, try sitting on your hands.

Easy Fondue

1 (10-3/4-ounce) can cream of mushroom soup
1 cup grated Swiss cheese
1 (2-ounce) jar of chopped pimentos
French bread, torn into bite-sized pieces for
   dipping

Mix and melt the first three ingredients together and pour into a 2-quart chafing dish.
   Serve with the bread and a green salad.
   Makes 4 to 6 servings.

Guacamole

2 ripe avocados
2 medium-sized tomatoes
1 bunch green onions or scallions, chopped
2 tablespoons lemon juice
1/2 teaspoon Tabasco sauce
2 teaspoons salt
Dash of garlic salt
1 (12-ounce) package tortilla chips

Peel and mash the avocados. Save one of the pits. Dip the tomatoes in boiling water for about 10 seconds, rinse in cold water, peel off the skin, and chop finely.
   Put the green onions, lemon juice and Tabasco sauce into the blender and chop for 3 seconds. Combine all the ingredients. Spoon into a serving bowl. Place the avocado pit in the center to keep the mixture from turning dark.
   Cover and chill until time to serve. Remove and discard the pit.
   Serve with chips for dipping.
   Makes 3 cups or 9 to 10 servings.

*I*f, in your listening, it seems that the other
person is speaking in some kind of code, it
may be that she is afraid of being rejected or
laughed at, so that she does not say what she
really means. She makes you responsible for the
effectiveness of the communication by having you
try to read her mind.

Help her say what she means.

Ken's Trash

1/2 of a 12-ounce box of rice chex
1/2 of a 12-ounce box of corn chex
1 (15-ounce) bag pretzel sticks
1 (12-ounce) can salted cocktail peanuts
2 packages white almond bark

Put all the dry ingredients together in a very large container, such as a clean dishpan. Melt the almond bark according to package directions. Pour over the dry ingredients and mix until thoroughly coated.

Dump onto wax paper on a firm, flat surface. Break into pieces when cooled. Store in an airtight container.

Makes a barrel full and can be frozen.

*H*ow *to listen so they'll talk: Nod and say,
"Uh, huh" and "Really?" a lot. Otherwise,
try to keep quiet. Allow feelings—any and all feelings. If this is about you, try not to be defensive.
Sit down, face to face, make eye contact, hold
hands, hug. Don't butt in. Don't judge, blame,
criticize, or preach. Don't try to fix anything
unless it's requested. You might ask, "How can
I help?"*

Mexican Fondue

4 cups shredded Cheddar cheese
4 cups shredded Monterey Jack cheese
1/4-cup all-purpose flour
2 teaspoons chili powder
1 large green bell pepper, seeded and cut into
    strips
1 large red bell pepper, seeded and cut into
    strips
2 cups stemmed and diced cherry tomatoes
2 large avocados, peeled and cut into thin strips
1 loaf sourdough or French bread
1 clove garlic, halved
1 (12-ounce) can beer
1 (4-ounce) can jalapeño peppers, seeded and
    chopped
1 (10-ounce) bag corn chips

In a 5-quart bowl, combine and blend the Cheddar and
Monterey Jack cheeses with flour and chili powder and
set aside. Wrap the vegetables and refrigerate until
serving time. Cut bread into 1-inch cubes, leaving crust
on. Wrap until serving time.

When ready to serve, rub the garlic along the inside of
a ceramic fondue pot or chafing dish. Add beer and heat
slowly, just until beer stops foaming and begins to bubble.

Gradually add cheese mixture, stirring constantly,
until cheese is melted and smooth. Add jalapeño peppers. Place on a candle warmer and serve with pepper
strips, avocado pieces, bread chunks, cherry tomatoes,
and corn chips.

Serves a crowd.

*S*ometimes, words hide more than they reveal. *Look below the surface words and ask about their deeper meaning and the feelings behind the words.*

Try to listen to what she's not saying.

It's great when you can sense what she's experiencing and reflect that back to her. This way, you can check to see if you're "getting" what she is trying to say, she's "getting" that you are listening, and you're helping her understand herself.

Nachos

12 Mexican-style tostadas
1 (16-ounce) can vegetarian refried beans
1 tablespoon cider vinegar
**2 tablespoons instant dried onions or finely-
minced fresh green onions**
Strips of jalapeño peppers
2 cups shredded Cheddar or Jack cheese

Place the tostadas on a large cookie sheet. Mix the beans, vinegar, and onions. Spread on the tostadas. Top with the jalapeño peppers, according to taste. Put the cheese on top. Bake at 400° for 10 minutes or until the cheese is melted.
Makes 12 servings.

Usually, when people no longer talk, they no longer care. They've closed up, shut down, and turned off. They've given up. Sometimes, the relationship dies long before the funeral actually takes place.

Better take notice!

Never-Fail Microwave Peanut Brittle

1 cup sugar
1/2 cup white corn syrup
1 cup raw peanuts
1/8 teaspoon salt
1 teaspoon butter
1 teaspoon vanilla
1 teaspoon baking soda

In a 1-1/2 quart casserole, stir together the sugar, corn syrup, raw peanuts, and salt, mixing well. Microwave on high for 6 to 9 minutes until light brown. Add the butter and vanilla and stir well. Microwave at high 1 to 2 minutes longer. Peanuts will be light brown and syrup will be very hot. Add the baking soda and gently stir until light and foamy.

Pour onto a lightly buttered, 13 x 9 x 2-inch cookie sheet. Let cool 30 to 60 minutes. When cool, break into small pieces.

Treat a confidence as a special gift. Trust is built slowly but is destroyed in an instant. Once the trust is violated, the door to communication slams shut for a long time, perhaps forever.

Try not to make it risky for him to be honest with you.

Pickled Mushrooms

1 pound fresh mushrooms
1 cup Italian dressing
2 tablespoons pimientos
2 tablespoons yellow onions, minced
1/2 teaspoon black pepper
1/2 clove garlic

Clean the mushrooms. Steam in double boiler or vegetable basket in a 2-1/2-quart saucepan for about 7 minutes. Put into a 1-quart jar or container. Mix the other ingredients together and pour mixture over mushrooms.
Refrigerate overnight.
Makes about 2-1/2 cups.

Toasted Pecans

2 cups pecan halves
1 tablespoon butter, melted
1 tablespoon Worcestershire sauce
1/4 teaspoon garlic salt

Make sure the nuts are clean of any pieces of shell. Place in a 2-inch deep baking pan so that the nuts can be stirred. Bake at 350° for about 20 minutes.
In a 1-quart bowl, mix the butter, Worcestershire sauce and garlic salt. Remove the nuts from the oven. Stir in the butter mixture. Return to the oven and bake for another 5 minutes. Stir and taste. If not quite done, bake another 5-6 minutes.
Be careful, as they can suddenly become overdone at the end of the cooking time.
Salt to taste while hot. Makes 2 cups.

*N*o *relationship can be nurturing unless all feelings can be openly and freely acknowledged and talked about, and all appropriate questions answered.*

A good family motto: "There is nothing that cannot be talked about in this family."

Breads

Banana Bread

2 cups sifted all-purpose flour
3 teaspoons baking powder
1/2 teaspoon salt
1-1/2 cups very ripe bananas, pureed in the
    blender
1 teaspoon lemon juice
2 eggs
1/2 cup shortening or 1 stick margarine
1 cup sugar
1 teaspoon vanilla
1 cup chopped nuts

Grease two 1-quart loaf pans. In a 1-quart bowl, sift the dry ingredients together. Put the bananas, lemon juice, and eggs in the blender together and puree.

In a 3-quart bowl, mix the shortening and sugar together until creamy and smooth. Add the banana-egg mixture and dry ingredients to the shortening and sugar mixture, alternating between the two and stirring after each addition.

Stir in the vanilla and nuts and pour into the loaf pans.

Bake at 325° for a little over 1 hour, or until a tester, inserted into the middle, comes out clean.

Makes 2 loaves.

*I*ntroverts usually listen more than they talk.
They take in more information than they give
out. Extroverts usually talk more than they listen,
so they give out more information than they take
in.

Try to create more balance.

Easy Holiday Pumpkin Bread

1-3/4 cups whole wheat flour
3/4 teaspoon baking powder
1-1/2 teaspoons baking soda
1/2 teaspoon salt
3-1/2 teaspoons pumpkin pie spice
1/2 cup butter
1/2 cup honey
3 eggs
1/2 cup molasses
1 cup mashed pumpkin
1 cup coarsely chopped walnuts
1/2 cup raisins

Grease a 9 x 5 x 3-inch loaf pan. In a 1-quart bowl, sift the dry ingredients together. In a 3-quart bowl, cream the butter and stir in the honey and eggs. Stir molasses into the pumpkin and add to the egg mixture.

Add the dry ingredients to the honey, egg, and pumpkin mixture. Add the walnuts and raisins and mix well. Pour mixture into the loaf pan.

Bake at 350° for 1 hour or until it tests done in the center, using a cake tester. When cool, cut into slices and serve with butter or whipped cream cheese.

Makes 1 loaf.

*S*ilence is okay. There are times when we think we should say something but don't know what to say. Those are the times when we say the dumbest things of all. Better to be silent. Be there. Bring food. Do the dishes. Give a hug. Say, "I'm sorry this has happened."

Foundation Sweet Dough

2 cakes or envelopes yeast
1/4 cup lukewarm water
1/4 cup shortening
1/2 cup sugar
1 teaspoon salt
1 cup milk, scalded
2 eggs, beaten
1 teaspoon grated lemon rind
5 cups sifted all-purpose flour

In a small bowl or cup, soften yeast in lukewarm water. In a 3-quart bowl, combine the shortening, sugar, salt, and milk; cool to lukewarm. Add softened yeast, eggs, lemon rind, and enough flour to make a stiff batter. Beat well. Add enough more flour to make a soft dough.

Turn out on a lightly floured board and knead until satiny. Place in a greased bowl and grease the surface of the dough. Cover and let it rise until doubled in bulk. When light, punch down. Shape into rings, rolls or coffee cakes and place into a shallow, 15 x 10 x 1-inch baking pan. Let it rise again. Bake at 350° for 25 minutes.

Icing
2 tablespoons warm milk
1 cup confectioners' sugar
1/2 teaspoon vanilla

Heat the milk and mix in the sugar and vanilla. Spread over the bread while it's warm, not hot.

The willow tree grows very fast but has shallow roots. The least storm or flood will wash the whole thing away. If our communication is shallow, then our relationship is shallow. It may not withstand the storms of life.

The bonsai plant is a tree that has intentionally been stunted in its infancy by removing its deepest and most important source of sustenance—its tap root. Likewise, our relationships will flourish only from communication at the deepest levels.

What are you not talking about?

Ham and Corn Muffins

2 eggs
1/2 cup melted margarine
1-1/2 cups buttermilk
3/4 cup frozen corn kernels, thawed
1/2 cup shredded ham
1 cup cornmeal
1 cup all-purpose flour
1-1/2 tablespoons sugar
1 teaspoon baking powder
1 teaspoon baking soda
1/2 teaspoon salt

Grease 2 standard-size muffin pans. In a 3-quart bowl, beat the eggs. Stir in margarine and buttermilk. Stir in the corn and ham. In a 1-quart bowl, combine the dry ingredients and mix well. Pour the dry ingredients into the corn and ham mixture and gently stir until mixed well. Pour into muffin pans, filling 2/3 full. Bake at 400° for 20-25 minutes.
Makes 12 muffins.

*A*re you bored with your marriage? Perhaps it's because your communication consists of a series of lifeless encounters. Are you angry at each other? Maybe it's because your communication consists of a series of conflicts, petty quarrels, and "make-wrongs."

Hot Gingerbread

1/2 cup sugar
1 cup cake flour
1/4 teaspoon cinnamon
1/4 teaspoon mace
1/4 teaspoon allspice
1/4 teaspoon cloves
1/2 teaspoon ginger
1/2 teaspoon salt
1 egg, beaten
1/4 cup molasses
1/4 cup melted shortening
1 teaspoon baking soda
1/2 cup boiling water
1 teaspoon vanilla
1/2 cup chopped pecans

Grease an 8-inch square cake pan. In a 1-quart bowl, sift together the sugar, cake flour, cinnamon, mace, allspice, cloves, ginger, and salt. In a 3-quart bowl, blend the egg, molasses, and shortening. Add the dry ingredients to the egg mixture and stir until smooth.

Combine baking soda and boiling water. Add to the first mixture with vanilla and stir until well-blended. Pour the thin batter into the cake pan. Sprinkle pecans over the top. Bake at 375° for 25–35 minutes.

Serve with whipped cream or vanilla ice cream.

If you make this recipe often, you can make it easier by making up the spice ingredients by the cupful and keeping it on hand, using 2 teaspoons per recipe.

*P*erhaps we nit-pick and nag about petty
annoyances because we are afraid to address
the significant issues. Remember how much de-
pends upon the quality of your communication.

Hush Puppies

1-1/2 cups corn meal
1/2 cup all-purpose flour
1/8 teaspoon salt
2 tablespoons baking powder
1/2 teaspoon baking soda
1 egg, beaten
1 cup buttermilk
1/4 cup canola oil
1/4 cup fried bacon pieces
1 onion, finely chopped
1 cup canola oil for frying

In a 3-quart bowl, mix all ingredients, except the canola oil for frying, and drop from a tablespoon into hot oil and cook until brown. Drain on paper towel.

Serve with fried fish and cole slaw, p. 183.

Makes 1 dozen.

*P*lease stop talking, commanding, ordering,
and correcting your dearest ones long
enough to find out who they are and begin to enjoy
them as persons.

The whole world is oppressed and lonely. Let's
let up on each other, reach out, and be more loving.

Lady Bird's Popovers

1 cup sifted all-purpose flour
1/2 teaspoon salt
2 eggs, beaten
1 cup milk
2 tablespoons melted shortening

Grease two standard-size muffin tins or 12 custard cups. In a 1-quart mixing bowl, sift the flour and salt together. In another 1-quart mixing bowl, combine the eggs, milk, and shortening. Put the pans into the oven to heat for about 1 minute. (Be careful; don't let the grease burn.)

Gradually add the flour-salt mixture to the egg, milk, and shortening mixture, beating for about 1 minute, until smooth. Remove the tins or cups from the oven. Fill to about 3/4 full. Bake at 450° for about 20 minutes. Reduce heat to 350° and continue baking another 15 minutes.

Makes 2 dozen.

A good quarrel is sometimes useful in clear-ing the air. But make and follow rules for fair fighting.

Avoid using the words "never" and "always." There is no such thing.

Name-calling and bringing up extraneous matters are off limits, too!

Refrigerator Bran Muffins

2 cups water
5 cups bran cereal
1 cup vegetable oil
1 cup sugar
1/2 cup molasses or honey
4 eggs, well beaten
1 quart buttermilk
5 cups all-purpose flour
5 teaspoons baking soda
1 teaspoon salt
1 cup raisins

Grease 2 standard size muffin tins. Bring 2 cups water to boil. In a 1-quart bowl, add the water to 2 cups of the bran cereal and let soak.

In a 3-quart bowl, combine the vegetable oil, sugar, molasses, eggs, and buttermilk.

In a 1-quart bowl, sift the flour, baking soda, and salt together and add to the buttermilk mixture. Add remaining 3 cups dry cereal and the raisins to the buttermilk mixture, then the soaked cereal. Mix well.

This makes a lot of muffins and can be stored in a covered container for up to a month. Bake all or part of the batter immediately, storing what is left. When ready to use, spoon into the muffin tins, filling 2/3 full.

Bake at 375° for 18 minutes.

*E*stablish a statute of limitations. Agree that, when one party has a problem with the other, he will bring it up within, say, a week. Once that time period has passed, it's too late. Time's up! So, handle it immediately and don't bring up old stuff. When a problem recurs, though, it's not old stuff; it's the same old stuff all over again.

Spanish Cornbread

1 cup buttermilk
1 cup yellow corn meal
1 cup sifted all-purpose flour
3 teaspoons sugar
1 teaspoon salt
1 teaspoon baking powder
1/2 teaspoon baking soda
1 egg
1/4 cup pickled jalapeño peppers, drained and
   chopped
1/4 cup melted shortening
1 (15-1/4-ounce) can whole kernel corn, drained
1 (4-ounce) jar diced pimientos, drained
2 cups shredded Cheddar cheese

Grease a 13 x 9 x 2-inch baking pan. In a 3-quart bowl, combine the buttermilk and corn meal and let stand for 30 minutes. In a 1-quart bowl, sift the flour, sugar, salt, baking powder, and baking soda together. Put the egg and jalapeño peppers in the blender and chop for 2 seconds. Combine the egg and jalapeño mixture with the shortening and the buttermilk-cornmeal mixture and stir well. Stir in the dry ingredients. Add the corn and pimientos and stir well. Fold in the cheese. Turn into the prepared pan. Bake at 375° for 30 minutes.
Makes 6-10 servings.

Tarrer Inn's Smashed Biscuits

1 package frozen jumbo biscuits

Place on a baking sheet and put into the refrigerator overnight to thaw and rise. Using a wide spatula, mash each biscuit down flat. Bake according to directions.

*H*ave you ever noticed someone who contin-
ues to bring up the same old complaint?
Chances are, she doesn't feel heard and, chances
are that she will continue to whine until someone
listens.

Zucchini Bread

2 cups sugar
1 cup margarine
3 eggs
1 teaspoon vanilla
2 cups shredded raw zucchini
3 cups all-purpose flour
1/4 teaspoon baking powder
1 teaspoon soda
1/2 teaspoon salt
1 teaspoon cinnamon
1 teaspoon cloves
1/2 teaspoon allspice
1/4 teaspoon nutmeg
1 cup raisins and/or 1-1/2 cups walnuts, broken

Grease two 1-quart loaf pans. In a 3-quart bowl, blend sugar and margarine. Add eggs and mix well. Add vanilla and stir in the zucchini.

In a 1-quart bowl, combine the flour, baking powder, soda, salt, and spices. Add to the egg and zucchini mixture and mix well. Add raisins and/or walnuts. Turn into the loaf pans. Bake at 325° for approximately 1 hour.

Test for doneness, either by using a cake tester or by pressing slightly on the top with a finger. If the indentation springs back, it is done; if it doesn't, cook for 5-6 more minutes.

Makes 2 loaves.

*W*hen two people have conflicting needs and wants, the intensity is diminished if each one is assured that his needs and wants will be considered, whatever resolution is reached.

Competition is fine in sports and games, but in a relationship, it destroys trust.

Remember, the loser usually gets even, if only in subtle, passive ways and in small increments of withholding love. So, in win/lose situations, there are, after all, two losers.

Breakfasts

Aunt Matsy's Foolproof Cheese Souffle

4 slices bread
1 cup shredded Cheddar cheese
3 eggs, beaten
2 cups milk
Salt and pepper to taste

Trim crusts from bread and place the bread in an 8 x 8 x 2-inch baking dish. Sprinkle the cheese over the bread. Combine the eggs and milk and pour over the bread. Let stand for at least one hour or overnight. Bake at 350° for about 20 minutes.

Makes 4 servings.

*T*echnical problems usually stay fixed for a
while. People problems don't. They require
regular maintenance and repair. Hang in there.
The reward is worth it.

Like automobiles, relationships require maintenance. For a group on a trip, getting to their
destination is the task. But the car needs maintenance all along the way and, if it breaks down, the
group will have to make a major stop to get it
fixed. The same goes for relationships. Otherwise,
you won't get to where you want to be. Better take
the time now to save time and more trouble in the
future.

Breakfast Casserole

2 slices bread
1 tablespoon butter
1-1/2 pounds bulk sausage
1 cup cooked grits*
4 cups shredded sharp Cheddar cheese
5 eggs
2 cups milk
1 teaspoon salt

Butter the bread on both sides. Place on bottom of a 13 x 9 x 2-inch pan.

Brown and drain the sausage and put it on top of the bread. Pour the grits over this. Sprinkle the cheese on top. Beat the eggs, milk, and salt together and pour over the ingredients in the pan. Refrigerate overnight. Bake at 350 degrees for 30 minutes.

Makes 6-8 servings.

*See recipe for Southern Grits on p. 81.

The grass is always greener where you water it.

What is the one thing that is more important to you than any other? What is your communication like in regard to that thing? Is your behavior consistent with what's important to you?

Cheese Bake

1 tablespoon butter or margarine
2 (4-ounce) cans chopped green chilies
4 cups shredded Cheddar cheese
6 eggs
1-1/2 cups biscuit mix
1 teaspoon salt
1 quart milk

Butter a 11 x 7 x 2-inch baking dish. Spread the chilies on the bottom of the dish. Cover with cheese. Beat the eggs, biscuit mix, salt, and milk together and pour over the cheese. Bake at 350° for 40-45 minutes.

Makes 4-6 servings.

*N*ame-calling and labeling communicate
nothing except hostility. They are attacks
that describe despicable character, not objection-
able behavior. They inflict hurt, while failing to
achieve change. Confrontation, to be effective,
brings about changed behavior without bruising
the relationship beyond repair.

Cheese Grits

1 cup grits
4 cups water
1 teaspoon salt
1/2 stick butter or margarine.
2 eggs
Small amount of milk
1 cup mild Cheddar cheese

In a 2-1/2 quart saucepan, combine the grits, water, butter or margarine, and salt and bring to a boil. Reduce to low heat and allow to simmer for about 15 minutes, stirring frequently, until the grits are soft, not stiff and not soupy. If they become too stiff, add a little hot water.

Grease a 2-quart casserole dish. Beat the eggs, adding enough milk to make 3/4 cup. Pour into the grits and stir. Pour the whole thing into the casserole dish. Bake at 350° for 25 minutes. Remove from the oven, top with the cheese, and bake for another 5 minutes.

For a zestier dish, use jalapeño Jack cheese or pepper cheese instead of the Cheddar.

Makes 6 servings.

If you need to confront someone about something that's bugging you, try to pick a time when you're most likely to get an acceptable response. Not when she's tired, sick or already angry. Wait until you cool down. Think about what you want to say and how to say it effectively. Ask for some time to talk about something. Be kind. Be prepared to hear her side and even to accept her defensiveness.

Corn Meal Waffles

1 cup corn meal
1 teaspoon salt
1 1/2 cups warm water
1 tablespoon canola oil
2 eggs, beaten
1/2 cup milk
1 cup all-purpose flour
1/2 teaspoon baking soda
3/4 cup buttermilk or sour milk

In a 2-1/2 quart double boiler mix the corn meal and salt thoroughly in the warm water, set over boiling water, and cook for 10 minutes, stirring constantly. Add the oil and beaten eggs to the mush.Stir in the milk.

In a 1-quart bowl, sift together the flour, baking soda and add to the mush. Stir in the buttermilk and mix well. Cook on a hot griddle or waffle iron.

Makes about 24 pancakes or waffle squares.

*H*ow to talk so they'll listen: If you put him on
the defensive, he won't be listening; he'll be
thinking of what to say to defend himself. Put
all judgment aside, at least for the moment.

Use this simple formula: Name (1) the offending
behavior, (2) its specific effect upon you, and (3)
your feelings about it. Be patient if he reacts nega-
tively.

In order to communicate without friction, communicate without blame.

Easy Poached Eggs

Eggs
Enough fat to cover bottom of skillet

Turn heat to medium high.* Place fat and eggs in the skillet, 2 or 3 at a time. Cook just long enough for the whites to coagulate. Add enough water to cover the bottom of the pan. Place a lid on the pan. Cook until the yolks are the desired doneness.

This method is a good replacement for fried eggs, eliminates the problem of parched edges, reduces fat intake, and makes for easy clean-up.

High heat makes the egg tough.

*I*s the behavior that's bothering you something
that is harming you in some specific, concrete
way? Is it keeping you from getting your wants
and needs met? Or, is it simply something you
don't like? Is your teenager's stereo so loud that it's
keeping you awake at night? Or, is it that you don't
like his taste in music?

Is this annoyance worth making a fuss over?

Ask God to help you sort out your part in the
mess.

Egg Omelet

6 eggs, separated
6 tablespoons hot water
3/4 teaspoon salt
Dash black pepper
1-1/2 tablespoons butter or margarine
Green peppers, onions, tomatoes, chopped,
    and 1 cup shredded Cheddar cheese (all
    optional)*

Turn the oven to 350°. In a 2-quart bowl, beat the egg whites until stiff. In a 1-quart bowl, beat the yolks until thick and lemon-colored. Beat hot water into the egg yolks and add salt and pepper. Fold yolks into stiffly beaten whites.

Melt butter in a 12-inch skillet or omelet pan, greasing the bottom and sides of the pan. Turn the egg mixture into the pan. Cover and cook over low heat until it is puffy and a light brown underneath.

Place the pan in the oven for 10 to 15 minutes, or until the top of the omelet is dry but not brown. Touch the top of the omelet lightly with the finger. If the top of the omelet does not stick to the finger, the omelet is done. Do not overcook. Loosen edges of the omelet, cut through the center and slip a spatula under the side. Fold 1/2 over the other and press slightly to make it stay in place. Serve at once.

Makes 4-6 servings.

*If you wish to add peppers, onions, or tomatoes to the omelet, sauté them in a little butter in the pan and set aside. Put the vegetables and cheese on top of the omelet after it is done, but before folding it over.

*E*ncourage talk about feelings. Teach the
vocabulary of feelings, the tools for talking
about them.

You are the sole authority on how you feel. Your
feelings are not right or wrong—they hurt sometimes and feel good sometimes—but they are
yours. Own them and don't allow others to invali-
date them.

Eggs Benedict

3 English muffins, sliced
6 eggs*
6 slices Canadian-style bacon or ham
Hollandaise Sauce**

Toast the English muffins. Poach 6 eggs to desired doneness.* Place meat on the muffins, then the eggs, and top with Hollandaise sauce.**

See recipe for Easy Poached Eggs on page 69.
**See recipe for Hollandaise sauce on page 199.*

French Toast with Orange Juice

2 eggs
4 tablespoons orange juice concentrate,
**   not diluted**
1/2 teaspoon cinnamon
1 teaspoon sugar or 1 packet sugar substitute
1 cup milk or reconstituted skim milk powder
8 slices day-old bread
1/8 cup canola oil
1/4 cup butter

In a shallow bowl, combine all the ingredients except the bread, oil, and butter. Dip the bread, one piece at a time, into the egg mixture. In a hot skillet, heat the oil and butter and brown the bread on both sides.
Makes 8 servings.

This is good with or without adding syrup.

*R*emember that feelings are not the same as facts. Feeling stupid is not the same as being stupid.

And remember, too, that feelings are temporary, not permanent. You may feel differently tomorrow, next week, next month. So, don't take quick actions based merely on feelings, as important as they are.

Low-cal Oatmeal

1 cup instant milk powder
2 cups water
1/4 teaspoon salt
1 cup quick-cooking oatmeal
1/2 cup raisins
Brown sugar

Mix the milk powder into the salted water and heat slowly, until almost scalding. Add the oatmeal and cook on low heat for 1-5 minutes, or until the desired consistency, stirring frequently. If it becomes too thick, add hot water. Add raisins and brown sugar.
Makes 2 servings.

Mexican Breakfast

4 green onions, chopped
1 medium green bell pepper, chopped
1 tablespoon olive oil
1 cup chili sauce (not picante)
1 cup shredded Cheddar or Monterey Jack cheese
4 poached or fried eggs*
4 toasted tortillas
1 avocado, sliced

In a 12-inch skillet, sauté the green onions and green bell pepper in the oil. Stir in the chili sauce and grated cheese. Place eggs on toasted tortillas, top with the cheese, and garnish with avocado.
Serve with refried beans, if desired.
Makes 4 servings.

*See recipe for Easy Poached Eggs on p. 69.

*A*nytime you speak from the viewpoint of your
feelings, you will be less likely to arouse
defensiveness. But avoid using the word "feel"
when what you mean is "think" or "believe."
Uncommunicated negative feelings stand in the
way of even having positive feelings.

Microwave Low-cal Oatmeal

1/2 cup quick-cooking oatmeal
1 cup water
1/8 teaspoon salt
1/2 cup instant milk powder
Powdered butter substitute
Raisins
Brown sugar or sugar substitute

Combine the oatmeal, water, salt, and milk powder in a microwave safe bowl. Microwave on high for about 3-1/2 minutes, stirring often. Watch carefully that it doesn't boil over.

Add powdered butter substitute, raisins, and brown sugar or sugar substitute. If it gets too thick, add hot water.

Makes 1 serving.

*D*r. Jerry Jampolski suggested that there are only two categories of feelings—love and fear—and that one either acts out of love or out of fear of not being loved. If your loved one is acting badly, perhaps she is acting out of fear—fear of not being loved—and is trying to get love. Try to give her what she needs.

Peasant Breakfast

1 (1-lb.) roll bulk sausage
1 tablespoon oil
2 cups hash brown potatoes, O'Brien style,
   thawed
6 eggs, slightly stirred
1 cup Cheddar cheese

Brown the sausage in a 12-inch skillet. Add the oil and potatoes when the sausage is about half done and brown them. Pour into a 2-quart casserole dish. Pour the eggs over the sausage-potato mixture. Sprinkle the cheese on top. Bake at 350° for 20 minutes, or until the eggs are set and the cheese is melted.
Serve with chips and salsa.
Makes 6-8 servings.

Scrambled Eggs
With baking soda to increase the volume

4 eggs, beaten
2 tablespoons milk
1/2 teaspoon salt
1/8 teaspoon baking soda (not baking powder)

In a 1-quart bowl, combine eggs, milk, salt, and soda. Pour into a greased 12-inch skillet and cook over low heat, stirring gently with a fork.
Optional: Chopped green onions, green peppers, bits of ham, or cheese can be added by sautéeing them in a little oil before adding the eggs.
Makes 6 servings.

79

*E*veryone is hurting to be understood, to be cut some slack. If you don't understand, just accept.

We're all lonely and we cry to be connected.

Southern Grits

1 cup grits
4 cups water
1 teaspoon salt

In a 2-1/2 quart saucepan, combine all the ingredients and bring to a boil. Reduce the heat to low and allow to simmer for about 15 minutes, stirring frequently, until the grits are soft, not stiff and not soupy. If they become too stiff, add a little hot water.

Serve with butter, margarine or gravy.

This goes good with eggs, ham, and sausage.

Makes 6-8 servings.

When a person is acting out, perhaps he is expressing something he can't verbalize.
Ask, "What do you need to tell me?"
Interpret fury as fear. Try to show him he is safe.

ℭasseroles

California Casserole

4 cups rice*
1 large bay leaf
1 cup chopped onion
1/4 cup butter
2 cups dairy sour cream (Fat-free works fine.)
1 cup cream-style cottage cheese
1/2 teaspoon salt
1/8 teaspoon pepper
1 (4-ounce) can chopped green chilies,
   including the juice
2 cups shredded sharp natural Cheddar cheese
Chopped parsley

In a 2-1/2 quart saucepan, cook the rice with the bay leaf. Lightly grease a 2-quart baking dish. In a 12-inch skillet, sauté the onion in the butter until golden, about 5 minutes. Remove the bay leaf from the rice and discard. Stir all the remaining ingredients in with the rice, saving 1 cup of the cheese and the parsley. Pour into the casserole dish and sprinkle the rest of the cheese on top. Bake at 375°, uncovered, for 25 minutes. Garnish with parsley. Makes 8 servings.

*See the recipe for Boiled Rice on p. 167.

B lame keeps wounds open; only forgiveness heals.

Has your offender done you any permanent harm? Is what you're upset about all that important? Can the broken thing be fixed or replaced? Is it something you can let go of?

Chicken and Dressing Casserole

1 medium onion, chopped
2 ribs celery, chopped
1 tablespoon canola oil
3 cups chopped, cooked chicken
1 package cornbread or herbal stuffing
1 pkg. chopped spinach, thawed and drained
4 cups chicken broth, or 2 cups broth and 2
  cups hot water

In a 5-quart Dutch oven, sauté the onion and celery in the oil until the onion is clear. Stir in the remaining ingredients and heat through. Pour into a 2-quart casserole. Bake at 350° for 25 minutes.
Makes 6 servings.

If you think you've let go of the thing that bothers you, but are compelled to complain to others about it, you haven't really let go, have you? Probably you would do well to talk to the person concerned.

Chicken Corn Bread Pie

1 (6-ounce) package corn bread mix
1/2 cup dairy sour cream (Fat-free works fine.)
2 cups chopped, cooked chicken
1 (7-ounce) can chopped green chilies
2 cups grated Cheddar cheese
1/4 cup mayonnaise
1 egg, slightly beaten
2 tablespoons chopped green onions
1/4 teaspoon celery salt
1/2 teaspoon salt
1/8 teaspoon black pepper
1/4 teaspoon cayenne pepper

In a 1-quart bowl, mix the corn bread according to directions on the package. Pour into a greased 13 x 9 x 2-inch baking pan. In a 3-quart bowl, mix all other ingredients together and spoon evenly over the cornbread.

Bake at 300° for 30 minutes.

Makes 6 servings.

If you say you forgive, but still don't feel healed, perhaps you need more time to process the hurt. Find a good listener.

Not only is it important to forgive, we must be able to put behind us what it was that we forgave.

Chili Casserole

2 tablespoons olive oil
1 cup chopped onion
2 cloves garlic, crushed finely
1 pound ground beef
4 teaspoons chili powder
2 teaspoons salt
1 (8-ounce) can tomato sauce
1 (12-ounce) can Mexican-style corn, drained
1 (15-1/4-ounce) can red kidney beans, drained
1/2 cup pitted, sliced ripe olives
1 (10 to 12-ounce) pkg.corn or tortilla chips
2 cups shredded Cheddar cheese

In hot oil in a 5-quart Dutch oven, sauté the onion and garlic until golden—about 3 minutes. Add ground beef, breaking it up with a spatula and cook until brown. Add the next six ingredients. Simmer for 25 minutes.

To serve, place a layer of chips on each plate, add the meat mixture, and top with the cheese.

Makes about 6 servings.

*F*or every criticism or complaint, be sure to give two words of love and appreciation. If you criticize without having given appreciation, it's like overdrawing at the bank, and we know what happens when we do that. Relationships can get overdrawn too, and often become bankrupt.

Fiesta Lasagna

1-1/2 pounds lean ground beef or turkey
1 (17-ounce) can whole kernel corn, drained
1 cup picante sauce (spicy salsa)
1 (14-1/2-ounce) can stewed tomatoes,
   chopped for 4 seconds in the blender
1 packet taco seasoning mix
1 (16-ounce) carton low-fat cottage cheese
2 eggs, beaten, or 1 carton cholesterol-free,
   real egg product
1 teaspoon dried oregano or a sprig of fresh
   oregano, chopped
10 corn tortillas
1-1/2 cups shredded Cheddar and/or Monterey
   Jack cheese

In a 5-quart Dutch oven, brown the meat, breaking it into fine pieces as it cooks. Add the next 4 ingredients and simmer 5 minutes. Lightly grease a 13 x 9 x 2-inch baking dish. In a 1-quart bowl, combine the cottage cheese, eggs or egg product, and oregano.

Place 5 tortillas on the bottom of the greased dish, overlapping if necessary. Spread half of the meat mixture on top of the tortillas, then all of the cottage cheese mixture. Place the 5 remaining tortillas over this and spread with the remaining meat mixture. Top with the Cheddar or Jack cheese.

Bake at 375° for 30 minutes, covered. Let stand for 10 minutes before serving. Cut into serving sizes.

Makes 6-8 servings.

*F*ear *is the main barrier to communication—*
fear of rejection, fear of not being loved and
valued. Sometimes, in telling the truth, we risk the
relationship, but withholding the truth is even
more debilitating.

Please try to be authentic. Say what you mean
and mean what you say. Try not to hint or beat
around the bush.

Ham-Hashbrowns Casserole

1 (2-pound) package frozen O'Brien-style hash
  brown potatoes, thawed
1 (8-ounce) package sliced ham, chopped
2 (10-3/4-ounce) cans cream of potato soup
2 cups dairy sour cream (Fat-free works fine.)
2 cups shredded sharp Cheddar cheese
1-1/2 cups grated Parmesan cheese

Lightly grease a 13 x 9 x 2-inch casserole. In a 3-quart bowl, combine potatoes, ham, potato soup, sour cream, and cheese. Pour into the greased dish. Bake at 375° until the top is browned, about 25 minutes. Just before the end of the baking time, sprinkle with the Parmesan cheese and bake for 5 more minutes. Serve immediately.
Makes about 12 servings.

Green peas can be added for more color and greater nutrition.

*B*e yourself, not a role, with your family.
When we behave as a role, we hear ourselves saying things we wish we hadn't said,
things we heard our parents say and vowed we'd
never say to our own children.

Let's break away from the patterns we learned
from our elders and create a whole, new way of
being with each other.

King Ranch Casserole

1 cup chicken broth
1 cup chopped onion
1 (10-3/4 ounce) can condensed cream of
chicken soup, not diluted
1 (10-3/4-ounce) can condensed cream of
mushroom soup, not diluted
1/2 cup diced red bell pepper
1 (14.5-ounce) can diced tomatoes with chilies
15 (4-1/2-inch) corn tortillas, torn into 8ths.
4 cups chopped, cooked chicken*
3 cups shredded Monterey Jack cheese

In a 2-1/2 quart saucepan, combine the broth, onion, cream of chicken soup, cream of mushroom soup, bell pepper, and diced tomatoes. Heat through, stirring often. In a 13 x 9 x 2-inch baking dish, layer the casserole as follows:
5 torn tortillas,
1/2 of the chicken,
1/3 of the soup mixture,
5 more tortillas,
the rest of the chicken,
1/3 of the soup mixture,
5 more tortillas,
and the remaining soup mixture.
Cover with cheese. Bake at 350° for 25 minutes, or until heated through.
Makes 8-10 servings

*See directions for Chicken in A Slow Cooker p.145.

*D*o you express your anger, giving specifics of what you're angry about, or do you act out your anger and leave others guessing what it's about?

Are you upset for the reasons you think you are upset? Look deeper. Focus your attention on your gut, right where your esophagus connects to your stomach. It knows.

Ask yourself, "What is it I'm afraid of?"

Mary's
Good-Enough-to-Be-Junk-Food
Casserole

2 pounds ground beef
1 large onion, chopped
1 (14-1/2-ounce) can stewed tomatoes, chopped
    in the blender for 6 seconds
1 (10-3/4-ounce) can cream of mushroom soup
2 (4.10-ounce) cans chopped, green chilies
1 cup shredded Cheddar cheese
1 pound macaroni, cooked according the
    package directions

Grease a 3-quart casserole dish. In a 5-quart Dutch oven, brown the beef and onion. Combine the meat with the remaining ingredients, saving 1/2 of the cheese. Pour into the casserole dish. Top with the rest of the cheese. Bake at 350° for 25 minutes
Makes 8-10 servings.

*A*ngry feelings are not wrong; they're just *uncomfortable and painful. Sometimes they are a signal that something's not right. Sometimes they are based upon faulty beliefs, irrational thoughts or unreasonable expectations. Check it out. Learn to express the angry feelings rather than act them out.*

Tamale Pie Casserole

1-1/2 cups yellow corn meal
6 cups warm water
1-1/2 teaspoon salt
1 cup chopped onion
2 tablespoons olive oil
1 pound lean ground beef
1 (14-1/2-ounce) can stewed tomatoes
4 teaspoons chili powder
1 (2 .25-ounce) can sliced, ripe olives
1 cup shredded Cheddar cheese

In a 2-1/2 quart saucepan, thoroughly mix the corn meal, water, and salt. Cook over medium-low heat about 5 minutes, stirring continuously until you have a soft mush. With a potato masher, mash out any lumps.

Grease a 3-quart baking dish. In a 12-inch skillet or 5-quart Dutch oven, sauté the onion in the oil briefly.

Add the ground beef and brown, chopping it into fine pieces as it cooks. Chop the tomatoes in the blender for 4 seconds. Stir the tomatoes, chili powder, and olives into the beef.

Pour half the corn meal mush into the baking dish. Add a layer of half the meat mixture and a half of the cheese. Layer the rest of the mush, then the remaining meat mixture. Top with the rest of the cheese.

Bake at 350° for 25 minutes.

Makes 5-6 servings.

*Please try to turn complaints into requests
such as, "Would you please...?" or "It would
please me if you..."*

*Try turning demands into preferences such as
"What I'd really prefer is not having to..." or "It
sure would be better if you..."*

*Try turning judgments into questions such as,
"What does that mean?" or "Please help me
understand."*

*Remember, happiness is not based upon getting
what we want.*

100

Tuna Casserole

1 (16-ounce) package rotini or other pasta
1 teaspoon olive oil
1 medium onion, chopped
1 rib celery, cut diagonally into thin slices
1 tablespoon olive oil
1 (12-ounce) can tuna
1 (10-3/4-ounce) can cream of celery soup
1 (4-ounce) jar diced pimientos
1 cup bread crumbs
Grease a 2-quart casserole.

In a 5-quart kettle, cook the pasta according to package
directions. Drain into a colander, rinse, toss with 1
teaspoon olive oil, and return to the kettle. In a 12-inch
skillet, sauté the onion and celery in the oil until the
onion is transparent.

Combine all the ingredients except the bread crumbs
in the kettle. Pour into the casserole. Sprinkle the bread
crumbs on the top.

Bake at 350° for 25 minutes.

Makes 6 servings.

*W*hen there is a question as to whom to blame, ask, "Who did what?" Then hold each responsible only for what he did, not for what someone else did.

Don't be made to feel guilty for someone else's behavior. What was your part? That's the part for which you're responsible.

Turkey Manicotti

6 manicotti shells
1 teaspoon salt
1 tablespoon instant minced onion
2 teaspoons water
1 (3-ounce) package cream cheese, softened
1 envelope sour cream sauce mix
1/4 cup milk
1 (3-ounce) can chopped mushrooms, drained
1 tablespoon snipped parsley
1/4 teaspoon salt
1/8 teaspoon pepper
2 cups diced cooked turkey or chicken
1 envelope cheese sauce mix
1/4 cup grated Parmesan cheese

In a 2-1/2 quart sauce pan, cook the shells in salted water according to package directions. Drain in a colander. In a small bowl or cup, combine the onion and water. In a 3-quart bowl, stir together the cream cheese, sour cream sauce mix, and milk.

Stir in onion, mushrooms, parsley, salt, and pepper. Fold in the turkey or chicken. Spoon into the shells. Arrange in single layer in 13 x 9 x 2-inch baking dish. Prepare cheese sauce mix and pour over manicotti. Bake at 350°, covered, for 30 minutes.

Just before the end of the baking time, remove from the oven, sprinkle the Parmesan over the top, and return to the oven for 5 more minutes.

Makes 6 servings.

The other three magic words are, "I was
wrong." Be willing to say you're wrong, even
if you believe the other person is more wrong than
you are.

When you apologize for some hurt or wrong-
doing, don't accompany the apology with excuses,
justifications, or explanations. Just say, "I'm sorry.
What can I do to make amends?" Then make the
amends quietly.

Overdoing an apology is a way of "turning the
tables," making the other party feel guilty for
saying anything.

Desserts

Beth's Lemon Chess Pie

2 cups sugar
1/2 cup butter or margarine
5 eggs
1 cup milk
1 tablespoon all-purpose flour
1 tablespoon corn meal
1/4 cup freshly squeezed lemon juice
Grated rind of 2 large lemons
1 unbaked 9-inch pie shell

Cream the sugar and butter or margarine. Add the eggs and milk and beat well. Sift the flour and corn meal together and add to the wet ingredients. Add the lemon juice and grated lemon rind and blend well. Pour the mixture into the pie shell. Bake @ 450° for 10 minutes, then 350° for 40 minutes or until a knife, inserted halfway between the center and edge, comes out clean. Serve at room temperature.

Makes one 9-inch pie.

*L*et's throw out judgmental shoulds, oughts, shouldn'ts, and oughtn'ts and replace them with words such as, "I'd like...", "It might be better if you..." and "I wish I had..."

Do you try to get what you want by manipulation or through the powers of persuasion?

Carrot Cake

1-1/2 cups canola oil
2 cups sugar
4 eggs
2 cups all-purpose flour
2 teaspoons baking powder
1-1/2 teaspoons baking soda
1 teaspoon salt
2 teaspoons cinnamon
1 (8-ounce) can crushed pineapple, with the
  juice
1 cup chopped pecans
2 cups grated carrots

Grease a 13 x 9 x 2-inch cake pan. In a 3-quart bowl, mix the oil, sugar, and eggs. In a 1-quart bowl, sift the flour, baking powder, soda, salt, and cinnamon together.

Add the dry ingredients to the oil, sugar, and egg mixture. Add the pineapple, nuts, and carrots. Pour into the greased pan.

Bake at 350° for 30-35 minutes.

Icing
1 (8-ounce) package regular cream cheese,
  softened
1 stick butter or margarine
1 box powdered sugar
2 teaspoons vanilla

Beat all the ingredients together until smooth and spread on the cake when done and cooled.

*P*lease quit scolding. It hurts the Soul. Just say what you want and need and what you'd like to have happen.

If you've ever been hit, you know how much violence wounded your Soul, so, make a vow not to wound your precious ones.

Crumb Crust

**1-1/2 cups fine crumbs (graham cracker,
chocolate, coconut, etc.)
1/3 cup sugar
1/3 cup melted butter**

Mix ingredients together and press into pie pan. The mixture will still be crumbly until you press it into the pan. Place a sheet of foil over the top to keep the crust from getting too brown. Bake at 350° for 8-10 minutes.

Dark Sweet Cherries Parfait

**1 (15-ounce) can dark sweet cherries, in syrup
2 teaspoons cornstarch
1 tablespoon sugar
1 cup dairy sour cream**

Drain 1/3 cup of the syrup from the cherries into a small bowl or cup. Mix in the cornstarch. Combine with the rest of the syrup and sugar in a 2-1/2 quart saucepan and cook slowly until thickened, stirring constantly.

When cooled, combine with the cherries and chill. When ready to serve, spoon the cherries and sour cream into parfait glasses or sherbet dishes, alternating layers. Swirl slightly to make a pretty design.

Makes 3-4 servings.

*W*hen you discipline a young person, always give information to go with it. Help her learn from her mistakes.

When you punish her, check to see if your actions are for her good, or if you are venting your own anger.

Easy Pecan Pie

1-1/4 cups pecans, broken
3 eggs
1 cup sugar
1 cup dark corn syrup
2 tablespoons margarine or butter
1 teaspoon vanilla
1 unbaked, 9-inch frozen deep-dish pie crust

Put the pecans into the pie crust and bake at 350° for about 10 minutes while collecting the other ingredients. Place all ingredients except the pecans and the crust in the blender and swirl until all ingredients are well mixed.

Pour the mixture into the pie crust. Bake at 350 degrees for 50 to 55 minutes, or until a knife inserted halfway between center and edge comes out clean. If the crust begins to brown before the middle is done, place a piece of aluminum foil over the pie.

Makes 6-8 servings.

If your behavior doesn't match your words, your words have little power. If you tell your child to stop jumping on the sofa and don't enforce it, he learns that your words mean little.

If you slap your child because he hit his sister, what does that tell him?

Egg Custard

2 cups milk
4 eggs
6 tablespoons sugar
1/8 teaspoon salt
1/2 teaspoon nutmeg
1 teaspoon vanilla

Butter 6 (3-inch) custard cups. Heat 1-1/2 cups of the milk in the microwave until scalding hot, but not boiling. In a 1-quart bowl, beat the eggs. Add the sugar, salt, nutmeg, 1/2 cup cold milk, and vanilla to the eggs. Slowly add the hot milk, stirring. Set the cups into a pan filled with 1/2 inch of hot water and fill with the custard.

Bake at 350° for 25 minutes, or until a knife blade comes out clean when inserted.

Makes 6 servings.

*W*hy?" *questions are not productive. Questions such as, "Why did you leave your bicycle in the driveway?" or "Why do you act that way?" only invite annoying excuses. "What?" questions get better results. Try, "What did you learn from that?"*

"What was your intention?"

Or "What's up with that?"

These result in more meaningful conversations.

Elaine's Lemon Ice Box Pie

**1 graham cracker crumb or baked pastry
8-inch pie crust***

Filling:
**1 can sweetened condensed milk
1/2 cup lemon juice
1 teaspoon grated lemon peel
2 egg yolks**

In a 1-quart bowl, stir together the condensed milk,
lemon juice, lemon peel, and egg yolks until thickened.
Fill the pie shell with the mixture.

Meringue:
**2 egg whites at room temperature
1/4 teaspoon cream of tartar
1/4 cup sugar**

In a 1-quart, non-plastic bowl, whip the egg whites
until they begin to thicken. Add the cream of tartar and
beat until they hold soft peaks. Gradually beat in the
sugar just until the whites hold firm peaks. Pile on top of
the pie filling, making sure the meringue touches the
inside edge of the pie shell.

Bake at 350° for about 15 minutes, or until the top is
golden brown. Cool the pie and refrigerate an hour or
more until it is thoroughly chilled.

See recipe for Crumb Crust on p. 109.

What is being said and done is not nearly as important as our interpretation of it. What meaning are you adding to what you see and hear? Is it an accurate assumption, or some fear from the past? When we add meaning to what another person is saying or interpret the motives behind his behavior, we are playing at mind-reading. Ask, instead.

Heavenly Cake

Cake
Yellow cake mix

Bake the cake, according to directions, in a 13 x 9 x 2-inch baking pan.

Glaze
1 cup milk
1 cup sugar
1 stick margarine
1 teaspoon vanilla
1 teaspoon butter flavoring
Whipped topping
1 (7-ounce) package shredded coconut

To make the glaze, bring the milk, sugar, and margarine to a boil. Remove from the heat and add the vanilla and butter flavoring. When the cake is done, allow it to cool for 10 minutes.

Poke holes in it with an ice pick about every 1-1/2 inches. Pour the glaze over the cake. When cool, cover with whipped topping and shredded coconut. Refrigerate until time to serve.

Makes one cake.

The word "honesty" has been overused and poorly understood.

"Constructive criticism" is seldom constructive.

Lemon Bars

1/2 cup butter
1/4 cup powdered sugar
1 cup all-purpose flour

Grease an 8 x 8 x 2-inch baking pan.
Cream together the butter, powdered sugar, and flour.
Press evenly into the pan.
Bake at 350° for 15-20 minutes.

Frosting
2 eggs
1 cup sugar
3 tablespoons lemon juice
1 teaspoon grated lemon rind
1/4 teaspoon salt
2 tablespoons flour

Beat the eggs, sugar, lemon juice, lemon rind, and salt together. Sift in the flour, stirring constantly to blend in well. Pour over baked crust. Bake at 350° for 20-25 minutes. Cool before cutting.
Makes about 32 bars.

How to differentiate between fair and unfair criticism: Is it about a specific behavior or about you as a person? Is it something that you can change? Is it something that can be helpful to you, or is it meant to hurt? Is it any of the other person's business?

Lemon Meringue Pie

3 eggs, separated
1/4 cup butter or margarine, melted
1 1/4 cups sugar
1/8 teaspoon salt
Grated rind of 1 lemon
6 tablespoons cornstarch
2 cups boiling water
1/2 cup lemon juice
1 (9-inch) baked pastry shell

In a 3-quart bowl, beat the egg yolks and add the melted butter.

In a 2-1/2-quart saucepan, mix the sugar, salt, lemon rind, and cornstarch. Add the boiling water gradually, stirring constantly. Simmer for 10 minutes, until thickened, stirring.

Add the lemon juice, and gradually stir this mixture into the egg yolks. Pour into the pastry shell.

Bake at 400° for 10 minutes.

Meringue
2 egg whites
1/4 teaspoon cream of tartar
1 tablespoon water
6 tablespoons sugar
1/8 teaspoon salt
1 tablespoon lemon rind

In a medium-sized, non-plastic bowl, beat the egg whites thoroughly, until they form peaks. Continue to beat while adding the cream of tartar. Gradually add the water. Gradually beat in the sugar, salt, and lemon rind, a little at a time. Pile on top of the filling and spread to the edges, making sure the meringue touches the crust.

Reduce oven to 350° and bake for 18 minutes.

*W*hen you're on the receiving end of criticism,
try not to be defensive. You may need to
hear what is being said.
Try to learn from any reasonable criticism.

Mama's Brownies

3 large eggs
2 cups sugar, less 1 teaspoon
2 tablespoons cocoa
3/4 cup hot, not boiling, canola oil
2 cups all-purpose flour
1/4 teaspoon salt
1 teaspoon baking powder
1 cup nuts, chopped
1/4 teaspoon vanilla

Grease a 13 x 9 x 2-inch baking pan.

In a 3-quart bowl, beat the eggs and sugar until light and fluffy. In a small bowl, mix the cocoa in the oil until dissolved. Add to the eggs and sugar mixture. Sift the flour, salt, and baking powder together. Fold into the wet ingredients. Fold in the nuts. Stir in the vanilla.

Bake at 300° for 20 minutes.

Let cool and cut into squares.

Makes about 2 dozen.

Love and Lemon Pie

*A*pologize for your actions, not for your exist-ence. There is a vast difference between making a mistake and being a mistake!

How to deal with unfair criticism: Simply say "Oh." or "Do you really think so?" Be light about it. Avoid sarcasm. In the face of constant criticism, try asking,"What are you hoping to accomplish?" or,"What would you like to have happen?"

Mexican Chocolate Cake

1 stick margarine
1/2 cup solid shortening
3 tablespoons cocoa
1 cup water
2 cups all-purpose flour
2 cups sugar
1 teaspoon cinnamon
1 teaspoon baking soda
1/2 cup buttermilk
2 eggs, slightly beaten
1 teaspoon vanilla

In a 2 1/2-quart saucepan, bring the margarine, solid shortening, cocoa and water to a boil, then cool.

In a 3-quart bowl, sift together the flour, sugar, cinnamon, and baking soda. Add the buttermilk, eggs, and vanilla to the dry ingredients, blending well.

Combine with the cocoa mixture, blending well.

Pour into the greased 13x9x2-inch pan and bake for 25 minutes at 350° or until the top springs back when touched.

Frosting
1/2 stick margarine, softened
1-1/2 tablespoons cocoa
3 tablespoons milk
1/2 box powdered sugar
1 teaspoon vanilla

In a 2-quart bowl, mix all the ingredients until smooth. Spread on the cake while it is warm.

*Words cannot be taken back. Be careful.
Sticks and stones may break my bones and
words will definitely hurt my Soul.*

Peach Crumb Cobbler

6-8 peaches, blanched, peeled, stoned, and sliced
Sprinkle of sugar
Sprinkle of cinnamon
1 cup sugar
1 cup all-purpose flour
1/2 teaspoon salt
1 teaspoon baking powder
1 egg
2 tablespoons butter, melted

Butter a 13 x 9 x 2-inch baking dish. Arrange peaches in the pan. Sprinkle with sugar and cinnamon.

In a 2-quart bowl, sift together the sugar, flour, salt, and baking powder. Add the egg and mix with your hands until crumbly. Sprinkle over the peaches. Pour the butter over the top.

Bake at 350° for 40 minutes, or until brown on top.

Makes 6-8 servings.

A child's sense of self worth is formed at a very early age by what others say to him about himself. Cruel teasing and thoughtless name-calling will affect him his whole life. Let's speak consciously, especially with children.

Pie Crust
Made with Vegetable Shortening

2-1/8 cups all-purpose flour
2/3 cup canola or corn oil
1/3 cup milk

Mix all the ingredients together.
Separate and shape into two equal wads.
Place a wad between 2 pieces of waxed paper and roll out with a rolling pen until the desired size and shape.
(This dough can be handled and pieced together.as much as needed.)
To place into the pan, remove the top layer of paper, lift the bottom one, turn it over, and loosen the dough onto the pie pan.
Bake both crusts if needed, or save one wad in the refrigerator for a later time, tightly wrapped.
Makes 2 crusts.

*S*omeone has said that jocularity is a socially
acceptable form of aggression. Sometimes we
say hurtful things in a joking way, so that, when
the receiver takes offense, we can dodge responsi-
bility by saying,"I was only joking. Where's your
sense of humor?" That's not fair. The hurt is not a
joke.
  Please try to be more aware.

Prune Whip

Whites of 6 eggs
1/2 cup sugar
1 jar Junior baby prunes with 1 teaspoon lemon
  juice added*
1 teaspoon vanilla

In a medium-sized, nonplastic bowl, beat the egg whites until stiff enough to form peaks. Add the sugar, a little at a time, beating until the mixture looks satiny.

Fold in the prunes and vanilla. Turn into an ungreased 2-quart baking dish.

Bake at 350° for 30 minutes, or until a cake tester or thin knife, inserted, comes out clean.

Serve with whipped topping. Serves 6-8.

Pureed apricots can be substituted for the prunes.

*N*urturing communication is based upon the assumption that the people involved care about each other.

Try to make at least one loving statement to each of your precious ones every day. Cut down on the corrections and suggestions for improvement.

Strawberry Shortcake

2 cups all-purpose flour
1/8 cup sugar
1 tablespoon baking powder
1/2 teaspoon salt
1/2 cup butter or margarine
1 beaten egg
1/2 cup, plus 2 tablespoons, half and half
2 cups stemmed and sliced fresh strawberries
1 (16-ounce) carton of frozen, sliced
   strawberries, in the syrup
1 pint heavy cream, whipped, or 1 (12-ounce)
   container whipped topping*

In a 3-quart bowl, sift the dry ingredients together. Cut the butter or margarine into the dry ingredients with a knife and fork or pastry cutter, so that it looks like coarse corn meal. Mix the eggs and half and half and stir into the dry ingredients.

Gently spread onto a floured cutting board. Roll out and cut into serving sized rounds. Place on a greased 11 x 7 x 2-inch cookie sheet.

Bake at 450° for about 15 minutes.

Remove from pans and cool.

Combine the berries.

Slice the cakes and toast briefly in the broiler or toaster oven, soft side up. Place a spoonful of berries on each half and add whipped cream or whipped topping.

Then put the other half on top with more berries and another dollop of whipped cream or whipped topping.

Makes 6-8 servings.

Try folding some sour cream into the whipped topping, according to taste.

133

*D*on't always go by the book. Follow your heart. To put more soul into your relationships, don't be so reasonable—be a little outrageous.

In the most "soulful" relationships, there is a minimum of criticism and trying to change each other.

Sweet Potato Pie

3 medium sweet potatoes
5 tablespoons butter
3/4 cup sugar
1-1/4 teaspoons freshly ground nutmeg
1 large egg, slightly beaten
3 drops oil of cinnamon
2-1/4 teaspoons baking powder
3 tablespoons evaporated milk
Unbaked, 9-inch pie shell.

Microwave the sweet potatoes for 10-15 minutes, or until soft, depending on the power of the microwave. Cool and scoop out the potato pulp from the peeling. Put the potato pulp into a 1-1/2-quart bowl, add the butter and mash until smooth. Add the sugar, nutmeg, egg, and cinnamon oil.

In a small bowl or cup, combine the baking powder with the evaporated milk and blend. Add to the potato mixture and whisk until velvety. Mound into the pie shell and spread evenly to the edges.

Bake at 425° for 10 minutes, then at 350° for another 45 minutes, until a knife, inserted halfway between the middle and edge, comes out clean.

If the pie shell begins to get too brown before the filling is done, place a piece of foil over the top.

Cool to room temperature before serving. Serve with ice cream, whipped cream, or whipped topping.

Makes one 9-inch pie.

The reason we often don't get what we need and want is that we don't ask for it. Hinting and beating around the bush just don't work. Don't expect others to read your mind!

𝕸ain 𝕯ishes

Baked Ham

1 ham, butt or shank end
1/3 cup prepared mustard
1/2 cup brown sugar
1 (14-ounce) can sliced pineapple
Whole cloves

Wrap the ham in aluminum foil, place in a roasting pan, and place on rack in the center of the oven.

Bake at 300° for 20 minutes per pound. Remove foil and take off skin and excess fat.

Mix the mustard and brown sugar together and spread over the ham. Cover with pineapple slices, pinning them to the ham with wooden toothpicks. Stick whole cloves in the center of each pineapple slice.

Place the ham back into the oven for 30 minutes. If desired, place it under the broiler briefly, but watch it carefully so that it does not burn.

Cool slightly before slicing.

Makes 12-14 servings.

*H*ow do you go about getting what you need
and want? Do you scream and yell, scold
and punish? Or, do you use the power of
communication?

When you give someone "the silent treatment,"
that's emotional abuse.

Guess what? Others don't have to change before
we can have peace of mind.

Beef Stew

3 pounds good stew meat, trimmed and cut into
  chunks
All-purpose flour
Canola oil (or half oil and half butter)
1 clove sliced garlic
12 ounces beer or red wine
2 cups sliced carrots
2 cups sliced onions
Water
Dash cayenne pepper (Optional)
30-35 small pearl onions, peeled
30-35 fresh mushroom caps

Salt and pepper the meat well. Dredge the meat in the
flour, making sure that all sides are well-coated.

In a 5-quart Dutch oven brown the garlic in the
shortening until crisp. Add the meat and brown. When
the meat is brown, pour the beer or wine over it.

Add the carrots and sliced onions. Add enough water to
cover the meat and a dash of cayenne pepper, according
to taste. Bring to a boil, reduce heat, and simmer 1-1/2
hours. Add mushrooms and pearl onions during the last
10 minutes. Add more water, if needed to increase
volume of gravy.

Serve with potatoes, rice, or noodles.

Makes 8-10 servings.

*I*f one of our loved ones tries to get what she wants by throwing temper tantrums and we let her control us by our placating or doing as she demands, we are training her in how to get her way. And she is training us in how to keep her from getting into a rage.

Try not to let yourself be manipulated.

Beef Stroganoff

1 pound lean ground beef
1 large onion, sliced
1 (8-ounce) package fresh mushrooms, cleaned
   and sliced
1 (10-3/4-ounce) can cream of mushroom soup
2 cups dairy sour cream (Fat-free works fine.)
1 tablespoon Worcestershire sauce
1 tablespoon catsup
Salt and pepper to taste

In a 12-inch skillet or large Dutch oven, sauté the meat
and onion together. Add the mushrooms and cook for 5
minutes. Add the rest of the ingredients and simmer for
15 minutes on low.

Serve over cooked rice or noodles.

Makes 4-6 servings.

*L*et's make home a safe and secure place
where there is love, understanding and
support, a place where each can be refreshed and
replenished to cope more effectively with the com-
petitive world.

Chicken and Rice

1 medium onion, cut into chunks
3 ribs celery, cut into chunks
3 carrots, cut into small chunks
1/3 cup water
1 medium-sized chicken, cooked and cut up*
1 (14-3/4-ounce) can cream of chicken soup
1 package chicken and herb rice
1/4 teaspoon sage
1/4 teaspoon thyme

Put the onion, celery, carrots, and water into the blender and swirl for about 6 seconds.

In a 2-1/2-quart saucepan, mix the vegetable mixture with the chicken, soup, herb rice, and seasonings.

Bring to a boil, cover tightly, and reduce heat. Simmer for about 20 minutes, without lifting the lid.

Makes 6-8 servings.

*See directions for Chicken in a Slow-Cooker on p. 145.

We might think of home as a base camp for mountain climbers. In the morning we go out to make the climb; in the evening we come back to camp where we can rest and be renewed for the next day's challenge.

Chicken in a Slow-Cooker
(practically fat free)

Buy a large roasting chicken and remove all the skin and fat possible.

Clean the inside, scraping out all the little organs from the inside walls with a stiff brush.

Salt inside and out.

Place in a slow-cooker or crockpot and cook on low for 2 or more hours. Do not add liquid, as it makes its own broth. The chicken can cook from 2 to several hours without burning or cooking dry.

Strain the broth into a separate container, place in the refrigerator, and later remove any fat that has risen to the top.

Use the meat for casseroles, salads, sandwiches, etc., and the broth for soups and casseroles.

Cranberry Chicken or Ham

6 to 8 chicken pieces or 6 to 8 thick slices of ham
1 (16-ounce) can whole berry cranberry sauce
1 envelope dried onion soup mix
1 (8-ounce) bottle Russian dressing

Place the meat in a 13 x 9 x 2-inch baking pan.

Mix the cranberry sauce, onion soup mix, and Russian dressing together in a small bowl.

Pour over the meat.

Bake at 350° for about 1/2 hour.

Serve with cooked rice.*

Make 6-8 servings.

*See recipe for Boiled Rice on p. 167.

*D*innertime is an opportunity for nourishing the Soul, as well as the body. It is a time for visiting, laughing, cherishing, telling of the day. It may be the only regular time for bonding of the family. Families that don't share this time together are cheating themselves and stealing from the future.

If, because of busy schedules, family time can't be in the evening, or even every day, try to reserve some family time on a regular basis, and make it inviolate.

Curried Beef

1 medium onion, chopped
1 large green bell pepper, chopped
1 teaspoon olive oil
1 pound lean ground beef
1/3 cup crunchy peanut butter
1/2 cup raisins
1/2 teaspoon salt
1 cup warm water
2 tablespoons curry powder
    (from an Asian market)**
2 tablespoons soy sauce
1/4 cup Spanish peanuts
3 cups cooked long-grain, white rice*

In a 12-inch skillet or Dutch oven, sauté the onion and green bell pepper briefly in the oil. Add the beef and brown.

Add the peanut butter, raisins, and salt.

Mix the warm water into the curry powder and add to the beef mixture, a little at a time, according to how spicy you like it.

Add the soy sauce and simmer for about 25 minutes.

Serve on top of the rice and garnish with Spanish peanuts.

Makes 6 servings.

*See directions for Boiled Rice on p. 167.
**For a spicier dish, use 3 tablespoons of the curry powder.

A "*warm fuzzy*" *is a statement that helps the other person feel good about himself and about you, as well. Give a lot of them. They don't cost anything and the return on your effort is bountiful. You can put them in lunch boxes, briefcases, suitcases, socks, and under cereal bowls. Little ones can learn to do this too.*

Curried Chicken and Rice
(Country Captain)

1 (3-pound) chicken, cut up, with skin and fat
  removed
2 tablespoons butter or margarine
2 tablespoons olive oil
1 crushed garlic clove.
1 medium onion, sliced into thin strips
1 green bell pepper, sliced into thin strips
1 cup chicken broth
1 teaspoon salt
1-1/2 teaspoons curry powder (from the Asian
  market, if possible)
1 stick cinnamon
1 dash of cayenne pepper
1/2 cup raisins
1 tablespoon cornstarch
1/2 cup water
2 cups hot, cooked rice*

In a Dutch oven, brown the chicken in the butter and
oil. When it is nicely browned, place it on a plate.

In the fat left in the pan, brown the garlic until crisp,
add the onion and green bell pepper and sauté until limp.

Add the next 5 ingredients to the pan.

Return the chicken to the pan and bake, covered, at
350° for about 45 minutes.

Remove the chicken into a serving dish. Add the
raisins to the sauce. Mix the cornstarch with the water,
stir into the sauce, and cook until slightly thickened.

Pour over the chicken and serve over rice.

Makes 6-8 servings.

*See directions for Boiled Rice on p. 167.

*Q*uite possibly, we don't think to write brief notes of appreciation because we have no idea how wonderful our expressions of gratitude feel to those who receive them. This is because we tend to underestimate our impact upon others. Believe me, the impact is great and the task is so simple that it requires no more than five minutes of our time and a few cents for postage.

Faye's Pork Chops a l'Orange

6 pork chops
2 tablespoons olive oil
1/2 cup chopped onion
1/2 cup chopped green pepper
1 cup carrots, sliced thin
1/2 teaspoon salt
1 (6-ounce) can frozen orange juice concentrate,
thawed

In a 12-inch oven-proof skillet, brown the meat in the oil. Add the onion, green pepper, carrots, and salt. Pour the orange juice concentrate over the meat and vegetables.

Cover and bake at 350° for 30 minutes. Remove from the oven, baste, and return to the oven and bake, uncovered, for 15 more minutes.

Makes 6 servings.

*L*etters have more "soul" than phone calls. They deal with more significant matters and they express more genuine feelings. They are put in a drawer and read several times. Some of the most meaningful ones are put away in a trunk or file somewhere, to be read years later. Let's write more letters.

Ginger Beef

1/4 cup fresh ginger root, finely grated or chopped
(For a spicier dish, use 1/3 cup.)
2 tablespoons olive oil
1 medium onion, chopped
1 green bell pepper, chopped
1 pound lean ground beef
1 (14-1/2-ounce) can stewed tomatoes
1 teaspoon salt
1 teaspoon black pepper
2 cups hot, cooked rice*

In a 12-inch skillet, brown the fresh ginger root in the oil until brown and crisp, as you would garlic. Add the onions and green bell pepper and sauté briefly. Add the meat and brown.

Chop the tomatoes in the blender for 4 seconds. Add the tomatoes, salt, and pepper to the meat mixture.

Cover and simmer for 20 minutes.

Serve over the rice.

Makes 6 servings.

*See directions for Boiled Rice on p. 167.

*W*hen you give a compliment, make it more meaningful by making it about a specific behavior or talent. "I really admire the way you handled that situation," is more appreciated than, "You're really smart."

Try not to use compliments to manipulate others.

Italian Meat Balls and Spaghetti Sauce

Sauce

2 (15-ounce) cans tomato sauce
1 can water
1 teaspoon basil
1 teaspoon rosemary
1 or 2 bay leaves

Mix these ingredients in a kettle or slow-cooker. Cover and simmer while preparing the meat balls.

Meat Balls

1-1/2 pounds ground beef
1 egg
1 cup bread crumbs
2 tablespoons water
1 teaspoon salt
1 teaspoon pepper
1/4 teaspoon garlic powder
1 tablespoon sugar
2 tablespoons parsley, chopped

Mix all these ingredients and shape into 1 inch balls. Place under the broiler for about 10 minutes. Turn and broil for another 10 minutes. Pour off any grease.

Put the meatballs into the sauce. Simmer for 1 or 2 hours in the slow-cooker.*

Serve over cooked spaghetti.

Sprinkle with grated Parmesan cheese.

*The secret to Italian sauce is to go easy on the spices and, instead, cook it longer and slower to allow the flavors to emerge and blend.

*L*ook, face-to-face, into each other's eyes. They are the windows of the soul. Don't grin, grimace, or talk—just "be with."

Take time to notice those important Souls in your life. We're so busy doing for them that we aren't present for them. Look at their faces. They won't be the same tomorrow. Give them more of what you are than what you have.

Jim's Easy Meat Loaf

1 pound lean ground beef
1 cup bread crumbs
1/2 onion, chopped
1/2 cup green bell pepper, chopped
1/2 cup celery, chopped
1 (12-ounce) bottle chili sauce
Salt and pepper to taste

In a 3-quart bowl, combine all ingredients and mix well. Press into a standard loaf pan.

Bake at 350° for about 50 minutes, or until the meat pulls away from the sides of the pan.

Makes 6-8 servings

Lemon Pork Chops

4 pork chops
2 tablespoons olive or canola oil
4 slices lemon
4 slices onion
3/4 cup catsup
3/4 cup water

Brown chops in the oil in a heavy, 12-inch skillet. Place a slice of lemon and onion on top of each chop. Sprinkle with salt and pepper. Mix the catsup and water and pour over chops. Cover and simmer for 1/2 hour or until the pork is tender.

Serve with rice or noodles.

Makes 4 servings.

A relationship is like a plant. We have to tend
*it regularly, though not continuously, or it
will die. We can't put it on the shelf and expect to
find it there weeks, months, or years later. And, if
you bruise it with rough handling, it may not
survive.*

New England Baked Beans

1-1/2 pounds dry navy beans
12 cups cold water
4 slices bacon, chopped into small pieces and
  fried until crisp
Grease from the fried bacon
1/2 cup chopped onion
1/2 cup packed brown sugar
1/2 cup maple syrup
1 teaspoon salt
1 teaspoon mustard

Rinse the beans and place in a 5-quart kettle or Dutch oven. Add 12 cups cold water. Bring to boiling and simmer 2 minutes. Remove from heat. Cover, let stand 1 hour.*

Bring beans to boiling, and simmer until they are tender, about 40 minutes. Drain, reserving the liquid.

In a 3-quart casserole or bean pot, combine the beans, bacon, bacon grease, onion, brown sugar, maple syrup, salt, mustard, and 1 1/2 cups of the reserved liquid. Cover and bake at 300° for 3-1/2 to 4 hours. Stir occasionally. Add more of the reserved liquid, if needed.

Serve with corn bread and cole slaw**

Makes 8 servings.

Or, just add beans to the water and let stand over-night, without boiling.
** See recipe for Cole Slaw on p. 183.

While breaking a promise is unacceptable, it's okay to renegotiate. But please don't make a promise at the same time you're aiming to break it. That's called "hidden agenda" and destroys trust.

Party Ham Balls in Brown Sauce

1 pound ground ham
1-1/2 pounds lean ground pork
2 cups fine dry bread crumbs
2 eggs, well beaten
1 cup fresh milk, or reconstituted milk powder
1 cup brown sugar, packed
1 teaspoon dry mustard
1/2 cup cider vinegar

In a 3-quart bowl, combine the ham, pork, bread crumbs, eggs, and milk and mix thoroughly. Shape into 1-inch balls and arrange in a 13 x 9 x 2-inch baking dish.

Combine the brown sugar, dry mustard, and vinegar and stir until dissolved. Pour over the meatballs.

Bake at 350° for 1 hour, basting frequently.

Serve as an appetizer or main course.

Makes about 75.

Sloppy Joes

1 pound lean ground beef
1/2 cup chopped onion
1 (14-1/4-ounce) can vegetable soup, not diluted
2 tablespoons catsup
1 teaspoon prepared mustard
Dash black pepper
6 hamburger buns

In a 12-inch skillet, brown the beef and chopped onion, chopping and separating the meat.

Add the soup, catsup, mustard, and black pepper. Simmer about 5 minutes.

Serve on the buns.

Makes 6 servings.

A weekly, monthly, or occasional family circle promotes open communication, creating more love and understanding than you can imagine. The children may not seem to appreciate this practice now, but later in life, they will remember them as meaningful times with the family. Have each member complete the following sentences, then discuss them, using all your best listening skills:

"I'm sorry about..."

"Could you...?"

"I'm worried about..."

"I like to..."

"I love you because..."

"Why don't we...?"

"I wish..."

Ted's Elegant Meat Loaf

2 cloves garlic, finely chopped
2 tablespoons olive oil
2 tablespoons butter
1 medium onion, chopped
1/2 green bell pepper, chopped
1/2 red bell pepper, chopped
1-1/2 pounds lean ground meat—beef, pork, and/or veal
1 heaping tablespoon tomato paste
3 eggs
2 tablespoons mayonnaise
1/2 teaspoon tarragon
1 teaspoon oregano
1/4 teaspoon cayenne
1/4 teaspoon basil
1/4 teaspoon cumin
Salt and pepper to taste
1 cup Italian bread crumbs

In a 12-inch skillet, sauté the garlic in the oil and butter until crisp. Add the vegetables and sauté, stirring constantly until golden brown.

In a 3-quart bowl, combine and mix all ingredients well. Press into loaf pan.

Bake at 350° for 50 minutes, or until the loaf pulls away from the edges of the pan.

Makes 8-10 servings.

This dish is good hot or cold, saves well in the refrigerator, heats up well and is great on sandwiches, cold.

You might ask your child, "What would you wish for if you had three wishes?" Then, listen carefully and sensitively to his answers. Take pains to draw him out on each of his statements. By doing this, you will have gained valuable insight into his general attitudes, values and outlook. From this base of understanding, you can teach and guide him more effectively later on. And he will feel heard and understood.

Noodles, Potatoes and Rice

Baked Noodles

1 (8-ounce) package egg noodles
2 tablespoons butter
1/2 cup chopped green pepper
1/2 cup chopped onion
1 (4-ounce) jar chopped pimentos
1/4 teaspoon salt
1/8 teaspoon black pepper
1 cup milk
2 eggs, beaten

In a 2-1/2-quart saucepan, cook noodles according to package directions. Drain into a colander, rinse in cold water, drain again, and return to the saucepan. In the same pan, add all the other ingredients and stir together. Pour into a 2-quart greased casserole.
Bake at 350° for 25 minutes.
Makes 6-8 servings.

Wℯ could have the children teach us what they are learning in school.

To keep youngsters out of trouble and away from drugs, keep them busy and keep them talking.

Camping is an inexpensive form of vacation and provides few distractions from family togetherness. When each family member has a chore and takes turns with the cooking and cleanup, he feels more like part of the team.

Baked Noodles Romanoff

1 (8-ounce) package egg noodles
1 cup cottage cheese
1 cup dairy sour cream (Fat-free works fine.)
1/2 cup grated Parmesan cheese
1/2 cup herb-seasoned bread crumb stuffing
1 teaspoon parsley flakes

Grease a 2-quart casserole.

In a 2-1/2-quart saucepan, cook noodles according to package directions. Drain and put the noodles back into the pan. In the same pan, combine the noodles with the cottage cheese, sour cream, and Parmesan cheese. Turn into the casserole. Sprinkle bread crumb stuffing and parsley flakes over the top.

Bake at 350° until brown, about 25 minutes.

Makes 6 or 8 servings.

Boiled Rice

1 cup long-grain white rice
1-3/4 cups cold water
1 teaspoon salt.

Combine the rice, water, and salt. Bring to boil, stir, cover, and cook over low heat for 20 minutes. Avoid raising the lid, as that allows steam to escape.

Makes about 3-1/2 cups.

If you want the youngsters to cooperate more enthusiastically, let them help plan and make decisions. Enlist their help in making up the rules. Give them a say in where to put things, how to arrange the furniture. They'll be far more committed when they've had input. Parents have veto power, of course.

If a family prays out loud together—not just before meals, but at other times, too—each will learn of the others' deepest thoughts, concerns, and hopes. Those roots will go so deep that no flood or storm will be able to uproot them.

Chinese Fried Rice

3 tablespoons canola or peanut oil
1/4 cup green onions, chopped
1/4 cup celery, chopped
1 (8-ounce) package fresh, sliced mushrooms
1/2 cup fully-cooked pork, shredded
1 cup fresh bean sprouts
4 cups cooked, day-old rice
2 eggs, beaten
3 tablespoons soy sauce

Heat the oil in a wok or deep 12-inch skillet. Sauté the onions, celery, and mushrooms. Add the pork, bean sprouts, and rice. Cook on high heat, stirring constantly for about 5 minutes. At the last minute, add the egg and soy sauce and stir.

Serve with additional soy sauce, according to taste.
Makes 4-6 servings.

You might consider, as a family, creating a mission statement such as businesses do. The statement could include what the family stands for and what it stands against.

You might work as a family to draw up some agreements, values, and standards that guide decisions and behavior, establishing the understanding that being a part of this family means we do certain things and we don't do certain things.

Fettucine Alfredo (Low-Calorie)

1 (12-ounce) package Fettucine noodles
1 cup skimmed milk
1/2 cup grated Romano cheese
1/3 cup reduced-calorie margarine
1/8 teaspoon salt
1/8 teaspoon pepper

In a 5-quart Dutch oven, prepare the noodles according to instructions. Drain, rinse, and return noodles to Dutch oven.

Over low heat, gently toss noodles with the skimmed milk and remaining ingredients until the margarine melts and the mixture is heated through.

Makes about 6 servings.

The best time to teach and train young ones is when things are pretty much on an even keel, with no one particularly unhappy or upset. That's when the family can talk things over rationally, help members make decisions and weigh alternatives.

Adults telling stories of their lives is a great way to teach.

Jesse's Spanish Rice

1 clove garlic, minced
1/2 cup olive oil
2 cups long-grain white rice
1 medium onion, chopped
1 medium green bell pepper, chopped
2 teaspoons salt
1 teaspoon black pepper
1 teaspoon cayenne pepper
1 teaspoon bouillon powder or one cube
1/2 teaspoon ground cumin
1 (6-ounce) can tomato paste
3-1/2 cups water

Sauté the garlic in the oil in a 5-quart Dutch oven until crisp. Add the rice and brown. Add the onion and bell pepper and sauté. Add the salt, black pepper, cayenne pepper, bouillon, and cumin. Add the tomato paste, rinse the can with 1 cup of the water, and add to the mixture. Mix well. Add the rest of the water.

Reduce the heat and cook, covered, for 25-30 minutes, stirring once during the cooking time.

Makes 8-10 servings.

Encourage your kids and support them in reaching their own goals, not your plans for them. As they grow up, be a consultant. Consultants observe, listen, record and write reports. They give feedback, make suggestions, and point out alternatives and the possible consequences of each. Then they back off. They don't warn, threaten, or nag. Sometimes they negotiate.

Macaroni and Cheese

1-1/2 cups elbow macaroni
3 tablespoons butter
2 tablespoons all-purpose flour
1/2 teaspoon salt
1/2 teaspoon freshly ground black pepper
1 teaspoon prepared mustard
2 cups milk
2 cups shredded sharp Cheddar cheese

In a 2-1/2-quart saucepan, cook the macaroni according to package directions. Drain, rinse, and return to the pan.

In a separate 1-quart saucepan, melt the butter. Sprinkle in the flour, salt, and pepper and stir. Stir in the mustard. Gradually add the milk, stirring constantly. Cook on low and stir until the mixture is thickened and bubbly. Add the cheese and cook until the cheese is melted

Mix this sauce with the macaroni. Turn into a 1-1/2-quart casserole.

Bake at 350° for 25-30 minutes until heated through. Makes 6 servings.

*E*xpect your offspring to be different from you
and have slightly different values. Don't
take it personally, as a rejection of your own
values. They need to "try on" different styles and
roles. Chances are, when they are finished, they'll
be much the same as you. If not, try to enjoy them
as "interesting."

Letting go doesn't mean not caring. It means not
trying to control something we can't control.

Potatoes in Sour Cream

4 medium white potatoes
1 cup dairy sour cream (Fat-free works fine.)
1 tablespoon lime juice
2 tablespoons butter or powdered butter
   substitute
Salt and pepper to taste

Scrub the potatoes with a wire scrubber in warm soapy water. Rinse thoroughly. Cut into small chunks. Place in saucepan with enough water to cover the potatoes. Cook for about 20 minutes or until the potatoes are soft.

Add enough water to keep from scorching. Cook another ten minutes or until the water has thickened into a sauce. Gently stir in the sour cream, lime juice, butter, salt, and pepper.

Makes 6-8 servings.

Rice Pilaf

1-1/2 cups long-grain rice
1/4 cup onion, finely chopped
3 tablespoons butter or margarine
1 (14-1/2-ounce) can chicken broth
3/4 cup water
1 (10-ounce) package frozen green peas, thawed
1 teaspoon salt

Brown the rice and onion in the butter or margarine in a heavy skillet. Stir in the chicken broth, peas, water, and salt. Bring to a boil, then reduce the heat to low. Cover and simmer for 20 minutes without lifting the lid, as that will let out the steam.

Makes about 8 servings.

177

*T*he best way to help your children gain self-esteem is to encourage and enable them to do some things they will feel good about doing.
Be a cheerleader.

Salads

Cauliflower and Pasta Salad

1 package twirls pasta
1 head cauliflower
1 (10-ounce) package frozen green peas
1/4 cup olive oil
2/3 cup grated Pecorino cheese
2 cups ham, cut into strips or small chunks
1 (4-ounce) jar diced pimientos, <u>not</u> drained
1/4 cup Italian parsley, chopped fine
Salt and pepper to taste.

Fill a 5-quart Dutch oven or kettle 3/4 full of water and bring it to a boil. While the water is heating, wash the cauliflower and break into small pieces.

Put the pasta and cauliflower into the water and stir. When this begins to boil again, add the peas and stir. Bring to a boil again. Turn off the heat and allow to sit for 5-10 minutes.

Drain. Put into a 3-quart bowl. Add olive oil, cheese, ham and pimentos, parsley, salt, and pepper and toss.

Serve hot or cold.

Makes 10-12 servings.

The best way to help your children develop courage is to allow them to take a few risks—not foolish risks, but ones they are ready for. And be there, praising them for having taken the risk, even when they fail.

The best way to give your children character is to be there for them as they experience failure and grief, not by rescuing them from the consequences of their choices, but by helping them learn from them.

Celery Stuffed with Cream Cheese

1 stalk celery, separated, trimmed, scrubbed,
and dried with paper towel
1 (16-ounce) carton soft cream cheese
1 tablespoon mayonnaise
1 tablespoon cream or half and half
1/3 cup finely chopped pecans, slightly toasted

Mix the cream cheese, mayonnaise, and cream together until smooth. Add pecans. Fill the celery ribs. Chill and serve.

Chicken and Apple Salad

2/3 cup raisins
4 cups cooked and cubed chicken
2 apples, cubed
1 cup finely-chopped celery
1 cup mayonnaise or salad dressing
1 cup finely chopped pecans, slightly toasted

Pour hot water over the raisins and allow to sit for 5 minutes to fluff them up. Drain. Mix all ingredients except the pecans and refrigerate. Add the pecans just before serving.
Makes 5-6 servings.

This recipe is great with packaged wild rice, cooked, using canola oil instead of mayonaise.

*L*et's be there for our children as they struggle with delayed gratification and disappointment, helping them grow from their experiences.

Let's teach them self-esteem based upon who they are, not what they have.

Let's teach them values, provide loving guidance, and worry less about having their approval. They need parents, not pals.

Cole Slaw

1 medium head cabbage
4 ribs of celery, tops included
2 bunches green onions
1 medium green bell pepper
4 carrots, peeled or scraped
3/4 cup mayonnaise or salad dressing
1/2 cup vinegar dressing on p. 213*
2 teaspoons celery seed
1 teaspoon salt
Sugar to taste

Cut the vegetables into chunks small enough to process in the blender. Save the carrots and chop separately.

Fill the blender about 2/3 full of the chunks of the vegetables without crowding and cover with water. Chop for 6 seconds, drain into a colander. The carrots will take longer, about 10 seconds.

Repeat until all the vegetables are chopped and drained.

Using a glass or cup, press down on the vegetables to squeeze out all the water possible. Put into a three-quart bowl, add the dressings and celery seed, and stir well. Add salt to taste. Add sugar if desired.

Makes 8-10 servings.

This dish keeps well for several days. If it acquires too strong a taste, add a little sugar and more mayonnaise.

*Or use 1/4 cup sweet pickle relish, not drained, and 1/4 cup sugar.

*L*et's love and respect our spouses and try to make it work.

Let's not forget to love each one for who he is, not what he achieves. To love someone unconditionally is to value him even when he doesn't make a good showing.

Someone has said there is only one kind of love—unconditional love. Everything else is approval.

Cucumbers and Pineapple Salad

2 cucumbers, peeled, sliced into quarters lengthwise, seeded, and sliced into 1-inch pieces
1 (20-ounce) can pineapple chunks, sliced in half
1/4 cup balsamic vinegar
1/4 cup syrup from the pineapple
1/2 red bell pepper, sliced into thin strips.

Mix all the ingredients. Garnish with the red bell
pepper strips. Chill and serve.
Makes about 6 servings.

Egg Salad Sandwich Filling

3 hard cooked eggs, chopped
3 tablespoons mayonnaise
2 tablespoons finely chopped celery
2 tablespoons finely chopped green bell pepper
2 tablespoons finely chopped green onions
3 tablespoons finely chopped green stuffed
    olives
1 tablespoon catsup
3/4 teaspoon salt

Cook eggs on medium just until boiling, then reduce to
low heat and cook for 15 more minutes. Remove from
heat, drain, and place into cold water immediately.
Put a double handful of ice into the water and crack the
shells, allowing the eggs to cool off in the ice water. Peel.
In a 2-quart bowl, mash the eggs with the mayonnaise.
Add the rest of the ingredients and mix well. Cover and
refrigerate for use as needed.

*C*hildren in shame-based homes are not held
accountable for their behavior. They're just
yelled at, insulted, and sometimes hit. They're not
required to clean up their mess nor make amends
for harm done, but they're never let off the hook,
either. Their self-esteem is destroyed, little by
little.

Children in respectful homes are not demeaned
for mistakes and destructive behavior; they are
required to clean up the situation, with
no further discussion. Then, they're off the hook.
Self-esteem is still intact.

Green Pea Salad

2 (15-ounce) cans young sweet peas, drained
2 hard-cooked eggs, chopped
4 ribs celery, chopped
1 medium green bell pepper,
   chopped
2 bunches green onion, chopped
1 (4-ounce) jar diced pimientos
1 teaspoon celery seed
Salt and pepper to taste
1/3 cup mayonnaise or salad dressing

In a 3-quart bowl, mix all ingredients. Cover and refrigerate for 4 hours or overnight.
Serves 6-8.

Pear and Cheese Salad

About 1/2 head iceberg lettuce
2 (14-ounce) cans pears
About 1/2 cup mayonnaise or salad dressing*
2 cups shredded Cheddar cheese
1 small bottle maraschino cherries

Make stacks of 2 or 3 leaves of lettuce and place on a large platter. Put a pear half on each stack of lettuce. Add a dollop of mayonnaise on top of the pear. Top with a pile of cheese. Place a cherry in the center of each pear.
Makes 6-8 servings.

*The Lemony Mayonnaise on p.207 goes well with this salad.

*W*here families expect perfection from each
other, failure is certain. When anyone fails
to live up to the standard, he is shamed. Shame is
about who we are; guilt is about what we've done.
Shame is usually life-long, worn like a suit of
clothes. Guilt is assuaged when we make amends.
    Wouldn't you agree that perfectionism is the
most toxic element in any relationship?

Rice, Bean and Corn Salad

1 cup long grain white rice
1 3/4 cups water
2 teaspoons vegetable bouillon powder or 2 cubes
1 (15-ounce) can black beans, drained and rinsed
1 (15-1/4-ounce) can corn, drained
2 green onions, chopped
1 red bell pepper, chopped
1/2 teaspoon dried cumin
1 chopped tomato (to be added at the last minute)

In a 2-1/2-quart sauce pan, cook the rice with the bouillon powder or cubes in the water. Bring it to a boil, turn down the heat, and allow to simmer for 20 minutes covered, without lifting the lid. Cool. Combine the rice with the vegetables and cumin in a 3-quart bowl.

Dressing

1/2 cup minced cilantro
4 tablespoons lime juice
2 tablespoons olive oil
1/2 teaspoon salt
1/2 teaspoon dried cumin
A few sprinkles of black pepper and cayenne

Pull the cilantro off the stems, rinse, and drain. Put into the blender with the other dressing ingredients and chop for 4 seconds. Pour the dressing over the rice and bean mixture.

Cover and refrigerate several hours or overnight. Makes 8-10 servings. This recipe keeps well for several days.

Add the tomatoes near serving time.

*H*elp *a young person see alternatives for his life. Teach him that consequences are inseparable from choices. And, according to his age and capacity to cope, try not to spare him the consequences of his own choices.*

Three Bean Salad

2/3 cup white vinegar
1/3 cup canola oil
1 1/2 cups sugar
1 (14-ounce) can butter beans, drained
2 (14-ounce) cans green beans, drained
1 (14-ounce) can blackeyed peas, drained
1 (15.25-ounce) can whole kernel corn
2 bunches green onions, chopped.
1 medium green bell pepper, chopped
4 ribs celery, chopped
1 (4-ounce) jar diced pimientos, *not* drained

In a 3-quart bowl with a cover, combine all ingredients, cover wih a tight lid and marinate for 4 hours or overnight. Turn over frequently to keep the dressing evenly distributed.

Serves a crowd.

*E*veryone needs her own space, unviolated,
her own section of the closet and drawers
that others stay out of. Daughter needs to trust
that no one will read her diary. Son needs to trust
Mother to stay out of his room, unless she suspects
something dangerous or illegal is going on in
there. Wife needs to have a telephone conversation
without having to answer husband's, "Who was
that?" Husband's privacy is violated when Wife
opens his mail. This is about respect.

There is a big difference between privacy and
secrecy.

Tomato Aspic

1 envelope unflavored gelatin
1/4 cup cold water
1 (10-3/4-ounce) can tomato soup
2 (3-ounce) packages cream cheese,
    broken into small pieces
1/2 cup green onions, finely chopped
1/2 cup celery, finely chopped
1/2 cup green bell pepper, chopped
1/2 cup green stuffed olives
1/2 cup mayonnaise or salad dressing

Dissolve the gelatin in the water. In a 2-1/2-quart double boiler, heat the soup. Stir in the cream cheese. When creamy, add the dissolved gelatin. Cool.

Add the onion, celery, green bell peppers, olives, and mayonnaise. Pour into individual custard cups or into a ring mold. Refrigerate for several hours until set.

Make a bed of lettuce on a large platter.

To unmold the aspic, carefully hold the mold in warm water, being careful to not let water over the sides. When slightly loosened, turn the aspic onto the lettuce.

Refrigerate immediately to reset.

Makes 6-8 servings.

*E*veryone is hurting for more praise, more recognition. It's so powerful when you say,"You did a great job cleaning the refrigerator" or "That was a thoughtful thing you did for our neighbor." Praise can seem manipulative when usually given for pleasing behavior and seldom given for just being. Think how good it would feel to hear, "I'm glad you're my kid" or "I'm glad you married me."

Turkey-Rice Salad

1 cup long-grain white rice
1 teaspoon salt
2-1/4 cups water
1 medium bay leaf
2 cups smoked turkey, chopped*
1/2 cup mayonnaise**
3 ounces smoked almonds, sliced
1 green bell pepper, chopped
1/2 head iceberg lettuce, torn into pieces

In a 2-1/2-quart sauce pan, combine the rice, salt, water, and bay leaf. Bring to a boil, stir, cover, and cook on low for 20 minutes. When rice is cooled, remove the bay leaf and combine with the remaining ingredients. Chill and serve.
Makes 4-6 servings.

Ham can be used instead of smoked turkey.
**See recipe for Lemony Mayonnaise, p. 207.*

If you act as if you are your spouse's mother, he will act as if he is your child. If you act as if you are your spouse's child, she will act as if she is your mother.

Try to relate as adult to adult.

Sauces and Dressings

Almond Sauce for Fish

1/2 cup slivered almonds
3 tablespoons butter
1/2 teaspoon salt
2 tablespoons lemon juice

In a small skillet, cook the almonds in the butter until golden tan. Add the salt and lemon juice. Pour over broiled or baked fish.

Makes 3/4 cup.

*C*odependency is a term that is used too much and understood too little. The extreme codependent is one whose relationships are based on her being more adequate than others. Because she has poor self-esteem, she needs someone who is less adequate than she to make her feel worthwhile. Out of the belief that we aren't capable enough, she controls and helps out, even if we don't want her to.

Try to regain your autonomy.

Hey, it's still okay to do things to please others.

Blender Hollandaise Sauce

3 egg yolks
2 tablespoons lemon juice
1/2 teaspoon salt
1/8 teaspoon pepper
1/8 teaspoon Tabasco sauce
1/8 teaspoon Worcestershire sauce
1/2 cup soft butter
1/2 cup boiling water

Put all ingredients, except the water, in the blender and blend until smooth. Add boiling water slowly as you continue blending. Pour into top of double boiler and stir continuously over boiling water until sauce thickens. Remove from heat immediately. Cover and refrigerate for use as needed.

Makes about 1-1/2 cups.

Use as a topping for asparagus or Eggs Benedict. It can be kept indefinitely in the refrigerator and may be reheated.

The counter-dependent person is one who says, "I don't need anybody. I can do for myself." He probably has never had anyone he could depend upon. Maybe he has been betrayed in the past and has little trust. Let's help him learn to trust.

Cooked Salad Dressing

1/4 teaspoon salt
1 teaspoon dry mustard
1 tablespoon sugar
2 or 3 dashes cayenne pepper
2 tablespoons all-purpose flour
1 egg or 2 egg yolks, slightly beaten
2 tablespoons butter
3/4 cup milk
1/4 cup cider vinegar

Sift the dry ingredients together into the top of a double boiler. In a 1-quart bowl, mix the egg, butter, milk, and vinegar and add very slowly to the dry ingredients. Stir and cook over boiling water until the mixture begins to thicken. Strain, cover, and refrigerate for use as needed. Serve over fruit salad.
Makes 1 cup.
For thinner dressing, use one egg yolk.

For Cream Dressing
Omit the flour and butter. Use cream instead of milk. Follow the same cooking instructions as above.

*A*s often as possible, treat your children as you would your friends. For instance, you wouldn't embarrass your friends in front of others or fail to introduce them properly, would you?

Cranberry Sauce

1-1/2 cups sugar
Grated peel from 1 orange
Juice from the orange
1/2 teaspoon fresh ginger root, grated or chopped
   very fine
1/4 teaspoon salt
4 cups raw cranberries
1/2 cup toasted pecans, chopped

Combine all the ingredients except the cranberries and pecans in a pot, and simmer until the sugar is dissolved. Add the cranberries and cook until they pop open, 5 to 10 minutes. Add pecans and cool.
Can be stored for several weeks.
Makes about 5 cups.

Cucumber Sauce

1/2 cup heavy cream
2 tablespoons balsamic vinegar
1/4 teaspoon salt
2 or 3 dashes of black pepper
2 cucumbers, pared, chopped fine, and thoroughly drained

Chill all ingredients thoroughly. Beat the cream until thick but not stiff. Continue to beat the cream while gradually adding the vinegar. Add seasonings. Fold in the cucumber.
Serve over fish.
Makes about 3 cups.

*C*hildren have the right to be children. While they definitely need to be taught manners, we make a mistake to expect them to behave as adults. They have the right to choose their own friends, under the guidance of the parents. They have the right to have some things of their own, according to their capacity to care for them.

Etta Yvonne's Apple Butter

3 to 4 pounds of apples, washed, cored, and sliced
1/2 cup water
2 cups sugar
1/8 cup apple cider vinegar
3 to 4 drops oil of cinnamon, or acccording to
   taste
1 to 2 drops oil of cloves, or according to taste

Place the apples in a large kettle or slow-cooker. Add water to prevent sticking and cook at low heat, stirring frequently, until tender. When cool enough, puree in the blender. Put the pulp back into the kettle or slow cooker. Add the sugar and vinegar to taste.

Cook for several hours or overnight on low heat. Add the oil, stir, and cook for 2 hours on high heat, stirring frequently.

Makes 2-1/2 to 3 pints.

*A*ccepting failure fosters creativity and promotes the maturing process. Let's help
children learn from their mistakes and develop
strength of character through their sufferings.

Lemony Mayonnaise

1/2 cup or 1 (4-ounce) carton cholesterol-free
  real egg product
1 teaspoon salt
1 teaspoon sugar
1 teaspoon prepared mustard
2 cups corn oil
1 teaspoon lemon juice

Put the egg product, salt, sugar, and mustard into a 1-quart bowl and mix thoroughly. With the mixer on low speed, gradually and slowly add 1 cup of the oil. Add the lemon juice in the same manner. Gradually and slowly add the rest of the oil. Refrigerate in a container with a cover.

Makes about 2-1/4 cups.

Note: This recipe does not do well in a blender.

Marinade for Beef

1 cup salad oil
3/4 cup soy sauce
1/2 cup lemon juice
1/4 cup Worcestershire sauce
1/4 cup prepared mustard
1 or 2 teaspoons coarsely cracked pepper
1 clove crushed garlic

Combine all the ingredients in a 2-quart bowl with a lid. Store in the refrigerator until needed. When ready to use, cut up 3 pounds lean round or chuck beef into 1-inch pieces.

Marinate for 24-36 hours before grilling or pan frying.

*F*or most of us, grief is a difficult process that
we avoid at all costs. But that cost is greater
than we ever realize. When a child loses a pet or
friend, it is important for us to be there for him as
he grieves, and not try to make his pain go away.

Mark's Grandmother's Barbecue Sauce

2 (32-ounce) bottles catsup
1 (15-ounce) bottle Worcestershire sauce
1 (6-ounce) jar prepared mustard
1 pound brown sugar
1/2 bottle Louisiana-style hot sauce (not Tabasco)
4 tablespoons liquid smoke (optional)
3 ounces bourbon whiskey (optional)

In a 2-1/2-quart saucepan, mix all the ingredients and simmer for an hour, covered. If the mixture gets too thick, add a little water. Allow to cool. Return to original bottles, using a funnel. Cover and refrigerate.

Orange Butter Syrup

1/2 cup unsalted margarine or butter
1/2 cup sugar
1/2 cup frozen orange juice concentrate, not
   diluted.
2 tablespoons fresh lemon juice

In a 1-quart saucepan, mix all the ingredients. Heat to boiling.

Cook and stir 2 to 3 minutes, until thickened and sugar has dissolved. Serve warm over pancakes and waffles. Can be refrigerated, covered, for up to 2 weeks. Reheat before serving.

Makes about 1-1/2 cups.

Give freedom to the degree a child can handle it. We wouldn't allow a toddler in the front yard alone, and we wouldn't leave a five-year-old at the park by himself. Widen their area of freedom as they can handle it. When they become adults, we worry about them, but we must back off.

Let's try not to use our children's lives to prove who we are.

Picante Sauce (Spicy Salsa)

1 (14-1/2-ounce) can tomato sauce
Pickled jalapenos to taste
1 medium-size onion
1 (14-1/2-ounce) can diced, stewed tomatoes
1/2 teaspoon salt
1/2 teaspoon white pepper

Put the tomato sauce, jalapenos, and onion in the blender and chop for about 5 seconds. Add the rest of the ingredients and mix. Refrigerate.
Makes about 2 cups.

Spiced Vinegar for Salads

2 cups white distilled vinegar
3 cups sugar
1 teaspoon whole cloves
1 teaspoon celery seed
1 stick cinnamon

In a 2-1/2-quart saucepan, boil all ingredients for 15 minutes. Cool and store in refrigerator. When ready to use, strain only the amount needed.
Makes about 4 cups.

•*See recipe for cole slaw on p.183.*

*W*hen we try to "get" another person to do a
thing by making him feel guilty, it's called
manipulation. Instead, ask for what you want and
be willing to take "no" for an answer.

There's nothing wrong with saying "no" if the
request goes against our better judgment. It's even
nicer, though, to say "yes," provided we won't
resent or regret it later.

Let's allow others the freedom to say "no," too.

Vinaigrette

1 clove garlic, minced
1/2 teaspoon salt
2/3 cup olive oil
1 teaspoon Dijon-style mustard
1/3 cup lemon juice
1/2 teaspoon cracked pepper

In a 1-quart mixing bowl, mash the garlic and salt together to make a paste. Whisk in the oil slowly. Add the mustard, lemon juice, and cracked pepper. Store in the refrigerator.
Makes a little over 1 cup.

White Sauce

3 tablespoons butter
2 tablespoons all-purpose flour
2 cups milk
1 teaspoon salt
1/2 teaspoon black pepper

In a 1-quart saucepan, melt the butter, add the flour, and cook over low heat, stirring constantly. Add the milk gradually, stirring constantly. Add the salt and pepper and cook over low heat until thickened, stirring constantly. Do not allow to boil.
Makes a little over 2 cups.

Optional
1 teaspoon grated onion
1 teaspoon dry mustard
1/2 teaspoon Worcestershire sauce

Add the dry mustard to the flour before combining with the other ingredients. Add the onion and Worcestershire sauce after stirring in the milk.

213

*A*utonomy means "self-governing." It means
that we make decisions based upon our own
values and our purposes in life, not upon others'
expectations.

It means we won't be manipulated into doing
what goes against our better judgment.

Soups, Chowders, and Stews

Broccoli Soup

1 (15-ounce) jar processed salsa cheese
1 medium onion, chopped
2 teaspoons canola oil
1 pound broccoli, slightly cooked
1 quart milk, or reconstituted milk powder
Salt and pepper to taste

Heat the jar of salsa cheese in the microwave until melted, stirring often.

In a 2-1/2-quart saucepan, sauté the onion in the oil. Chop the broccoli with the milk in the blender briefly. Place all ingredients in the saucepan and simmer, stirring frequently. Do not allow it to boil. Add salt and pepper.

Makes 4-6 servings.

How not to be opinionated: Avoid stating what is merely your opinion as if it's a fact.

Do you confuse what is merely your opinion with who you are?

Do you allow differences of opinion to keep you apart from another?

Try to allow others to have their opinions too, and don't make them wrong if they take a different position.

Chicken Chowder

1 medium-sized chicken
3 or 4 celery tops
1-1/2 teaspoons salt
8 peppercorns
1 bay leaf
1/2 cup finely chopped onion
1 tablespoon canola oil
1 teaspoon curry powder from an Asian
   market (optional)
2 (16-ounce) cans cream-style corn
1 cup half and half, cream or liquid non-dairy
   creamer
1 (16-ounce) can chicken broth, plus broth from
   cooking the chicken
Black pepper to taste

Cook the chicken with the celery tops, salt, peppercorns, and bay leaf.* When the chicken is done, discard
the celery tops, peppercorns, and bay leaf.

Strain the broth and pour into a container separate
from the chicken and refrigerate. Cool the chicken and
dice.

In a Dutch oven sauté the onion in the oil. Add the
curry powder to the onions and cook 5 minutes longer on
low.

Remove the broth from the refrigerator and discard
any fat. Stir the chicken, corn, cream, and broth into
the onion mixture. Add the black pepper. Simmer until
the mixture is hot.

Makes 6-8 servings.

*See directions for Chicken in a Slow Cooker on page 145.

*D*o you buy the notion that to do something to please another is giving in?

Chicken Tortilla Soup

1 (28-ounce) can stewed tomatoes
1 medium onion, cut into chunks
1 tablespoon pickled jalapeño peppers,
   with the vinegar
1 cup fresh cilantro, washed and pulled
   from stem.
2 cups cooked chicken, diced*
Broth from the cooked chicken
2 (14-1/2-ounce) cans chicken broth
1 (4.5-ounce) can chopped green chilies
4 corn tortillas, torn into bite-sized pieces
1/2 teaspoon cumin
4 cups shredded Cheddar and Jack cheese

Chop the stewed tomatoes, onion, jalapeño peppers, and cilantro in the blender for 10 seconds. Put all the ingredients except the cheese into a 5-quart Dutch oven. Simmer for 30 minutes. To serve, ladle into bowls and top with mounds of cheese.

Makes about 2 quarts.

Option: Add one 15-ounce can of whole kernel corn.

See directions for Chicken in a Slow Cooker on page 145.

*H*ave you ever noticed the price we pay in order to be right? Can't you see how we sacrifice friendships, relationships, happiness, and peace of mind in order to be "one up"?

Corn Chowder

4 strips bacon, chopped into small pieces
1 medium onion, chopped
2 medium potatoes, peeled and
   chopped, or 2 cups frozen hash browns
2 cups water
2 (15-ounce) ounce cans cream style corn
1 cup fresh milk or 1/2 cup milk powder,
   mixed in the blender with 1 cup water
4 tablespoons butter
Salt and pepper to taste

In a 5-quart Dutch oven, brown the bacon until almost crisp. Add the onion and sauté it with the bacon. Add the potatoes and 2 cups water and cook until the potatoes are mushy. Add the corn, milk, butter, salt, and pepper.
Makes 4-6 servings.

Optional: For a zestier soup, put 1 heaping tablespoon pickled japenos in the blender with the milk and chop.

*A*s a parent or supervisor at work, are you operating out of power and control, or out of effective communication?

Give up trying to control. Be a leader, not a boss. Rely on influence rather than authority. Yes, you need to have authority, but when you have to use it instead of influence, there has been a lack of influence and a failure in the communication.

Replace the need to control with the desire to love.

Cream of Onion Soup

2 large, mild onions, sliced thin
1/4 cup butter or margarine
4 cups chicken broth
1 cup milk or cream
1 tablespoon chopped green bell pepper
1/4 cup grated Swiss cheese

In a 2-1/2-quart saucepan, cook the onions in the butter until they are clear, about 10 minutes, stirring constantly. Add the chicken broth. Cook slowly for about 30 minutes. Add the milk or cream. Just before serving, add the green bell pepper and grated cheese.
Makes 4-5 servings.

Faye's Taco Soup

1 pound ground turkey or lean ground beef
1/2 medium onion, chopped
1 (15-ounce) can pinto beans, drained
1 (15-ounce) can kidney beans, drained
1 (15-ounce) can hominy (the yellow kind, with
    green bell pepper), drained
1 (10-ounce) can tomatoes with peppers or stewed
    tomatoes
1 (15-ounce) can whole kernel corn, drained
1 package taco seasoning mix
1 package ranch dressing mix
2 cups water

In a 5-quart Dutch oven, sauté the meat and onion.
Add contents of cans to the meat in the kettle.
Add the seasonings and water.
Mix well, simmer for 35 minutes.
Makes 8-10 servings.

*L*et's stop the lying. In our homes, schools,
workplaces, government. If not all that, then,
at least, with ourselves.

French Onion Soup

4 onions, sliced thin
2 tablespoons butter
1 teaspoon flour
1 quart beef broth
Salt and pepper to taste

In a 2-1/2-quart saucepan, brown the onions in the butter until clear. Add flour slowly and gradually, stirring constantly. Add the beef broth gradually and stir. Add the salt and pepper. Simmer for 20 minutes.
Makes 4-5 servings.

Glenda's Pizza Soup

2 rolls bulk Italian sausage
1/2 onion, chopped
1 small carton fresh mushrooms
1 large green pepper, chopped
2 (14-1/2-ounce) cans stewed tomatoes
1 1/2 cups Ragu traditional marinara sauce
2 (14-1/2 ounce) cans chicken broth.
25 or more slices pepperoni
2 cups shredded zucchini
1 cup shredded Parmesan cheese
1/2 cup sliced black olives

In a 5-quart Dutch oven, brown the sausage. Add the onion and mushrooms and sauté them together with the sausage. Add the other ingredients, except the zucchini, olives, and cheese and simmer for 25 minutes. Add the zucchini and simmer for 1 minute.
To serve, pour into serving bowls and place a mound of cheese and olives on top.
Serves a crowd.

*L*et's teach old-fashioned integrity. Character is the way we behave when no one is looking. Let's teach our children to do the right thing, not out of fear of being caught and punished for doing the wrong thing, but to do the right thing because society demands it, God commands it, and, because, after all, it's the only way that life works.

Hearty Bean Soup

3 cloves garlic, minced
3 tablespoons olive oil
2 pounds ground beef
2 onions, chopped
1 (14-ounce) can red kidney beans
1 teaspoon oregano
2 tablespoons chili powder
4 teaspoons sugar
1 teaspoon salt
2 tablespoons apple cider vinegar
1 (4-ounce) jar diced pimentos
1 (15-ounce) can tomato sauce
1 (15-ounce) can stewed tomatoes
4 cups water
Black pepper to taste
1/2 cabbage, shredded

In 5-quart Dutch oven, brown the garlic in olive oil. Add ground beef and brown, chopping it into small pieces as it cooks. Add onions and sauté until clear. Add the remaining ingredients except the cabbage and simmer half an hour. Add the cabbage and cook five minutes longer. Makes 12 very hearty servings.

Serve with carrot and celery sticks, and saltine crackers.

*A*re your behaviors in line with your values? What are your children learning from you about integrity?

Remember, children learn what they live and see, not what they are told.

Mexican Vegetable Soup

1 pound ground beef
1 1/4 ounce package taco seasoning mix
1 (46-ounce) can tomato juice
1 (15-ounce) can chili beans
1 (16-ounce) package frozen mixed vegetables
1 (12-ounce) can tomato paste
2 cups corn chips, crushed
8 ounces shredded Cheddar cheese

In a 5-quart Dutch oven, brown the ground beef. Add taco seasoning mix, tomato juice, chili beans, frozen vegetables, and tomato paste and mix well. Bring just to a boil. Reduce heat and simmer uncovered for 20-25 minutes or until vegetables are tender, stirring occasionally. Top each serving with corn chips and cheese.
Makes 11 servings.

*A*re alcohol and drugs becoming the center
of your life? If chemicals are causing
problems, then you have a chemical problem.
Please, please, get help now.

Vegetable Soup

1 pound stew beef, cut into small slices
2 tablespoons olive oil
Handful of beef marrow bones
2 cups water
1 large bay leaf
1 (28-ounce) can stewed tomatoes
1 large onion, cut into chunks
4 carrots, cut into chunks
4 ribs celery, cut into chunks
1 (15-1/4 ounce) can whole kernel corn
2 (15-1/4 ounce) cans cut green beans
Salt and pepper to taste

In a 5-quart Dutch oven, brown the stew meat in the oil. Add the bones and water to the meat and boil on low with the bay leaf, for 1/2 hour. Chop the stewed tomatoes, onion, carrots, and celery in the blender for 6 seconds and add to the meat. Add the corn, beans, salt, and pepper.

Simmer for 1 hour. Remove the bay leaf and bones. Serve with saltine crackers.

Makes about 3 quarts.

*A*n addiction is anything we think we have to lie about.

Vegetables

Asparagus

2 bunches fresh asparagus
4 tablespoons butter
1 lemon
Salt and pepper to taste

To determine how much of the stalk to discard, hold each stalk by the bottom end with one hand and about half-way down with the other hand. Bend until it snaps. Wash and drain.

Place the asparagus in a microwave-safe dish and cook on high for 5 minutes. Place on a serving dish. Drizzle the butter and lemon juice on top.* Add salt and pepper to taste.

Makes 4 servings.

Or top with the Hollandaise Sauce on p 199.

*C*hildren need fathers in their lives. When couples divorce, the children need to continue a close relationship with their father, even if he does not meet ideal standards.

Divorced parents harm the children when they trash each other.

Cabbage and Noodles

**1 (8-ounce) package broad noodles, boiled and
   drained**
1 teaspoon olive oil
1 large cabbage
3/4 cup butter
1 teaspoon salt
Freshly ground black pepper
2 tablespoons poppy seed

In a 2-1/2-quart saucepan, cook the noodles according
to package directions. Drain into a colander, return to
the saucepan and toss with the olive oil. Set aside. Chop
the cabbage.

In a 5-quart Dutch oven, place enough water to cover
the cabbage. Cook on high for about 5 minutes. Drain
into a colander and return to the Dutch oven.

Sauté the cooked cabbage in 1/2 cup of the butter over
low heat for 15 minutes, stirring frequently. Season with
the salt, freshly ground black pepper, and poppy seed.
Combine the noodles with the cabbage and the remaining 1/4 cup of the butter. Mix thoroughly and serve hot.

Makes 6-8 servings.

*P*erhaps the reason that divorcing couples
   often become so vicious is that they begin to
vent feelings that they have saved up for years.
Out of reluctance to talk about feelings for fear of
causing trouble, they have withheld. And, once the
relationship is over, they let each other have it with
both barrels, to the detriment of all. Better to take
care of things as they come up.

Corn Pudding

3 eggs
1 tablespoon grated onion
1/4 cup green pepper, chopped fine
1 (4-ounce) jar pimientos
1 teaspoon salt
1 (15-ounce) can cream style corn
2 tablespoons sugar
2 cups scalded milk
Paprika

In a medium-size bowl, beat the eggs. Combine all the ingredients, except the paprika, in the bowl and pour into a buttered, 2-quart casserole. Sprinkle with paprika. Bake at 350° for about 50 minutes or until set. Makes 6-8 servings.

Creamed Onions

3 cups sliced onion
1/4 cup butter, melted
2 tablespoons all-purpose flour
1 teaspoon salt
1/4 teaspoon dried thyme, crushed
Dash of pepper
1 cup milk

Place the onion in a 1-quart saucepan with enough salted water to cover it. Cook, until tender, 20-25 minutes. Drain into a colander.

In the same pan, mix the butter, flour, salt, thyme, and a dash of pepper. Blend in the milk slowly. Cook, stirring constantly, until thickened and bubbly. Stir in the onion slices. Heat through.
Makes 6-8 servings.

If you say you love someone, surely you want the best for that person, at least what you would want for yourself. Surely you wouldn't want to hurt him.

Someone has said that love is not just a feeling, that it's doing the loving thing, even when we're not feeling loving at all.

Easy Creamed Spinach

1 (10-ounce) package frozen spinach, thawed
1/4 cup butter, melted
2 tablespoons all-purpose flour
1 teaspoon salt
Dash of pepper
1 cup milk
1 tablespoon Worcestershire sauce

In a 2-1/2-quart saucepan, cook the spinach according to package directions. Drain into a colander. In the same pan, mix the butter, flour, salt, and pepper. Blend in the milk slowly, stirring constantly, and cook until thickened. Stir in the spinach and Worcestershire sauce. Makes 2-3 servings.

Garlic Green Beans

2 pounds fresh green beans or 2 packages frozen green beans, thawed.
1 cup water
1 teaspoon salt
1/4 cup butter or margarine
4 cloves garlic, minced
1/4 teaspoon lemon pepper seasoning
1/4 teaspoon herb seasoning
1/3 cup chopped fresh parsley

Wash and snap the beans. In a 5-quart Dutch oven, simmer the beans for 10 minutes in the salted water. Drain into a colander. Melt the butter in the Dutch oven. Add the garlic and cook until tender. Stir in the lemon pepper and herb seasoning. Add the beans and cook, stirring occasionally, for 10 minutes, or until thoroughly heated. Spoon into a serving dish. Sprinkle with parsley. Makes 6-8 servings.

*H*ealthy self-esteem comes from doing something good.
We would feel better about ourselves by doing
something better.
We could quit doing the things we feel bad about.
We could do more of the things we don't want to
do.

Glazed Carrots

2 pounds carrots, either whole carrots or baby
  carrots
1/3 cup brown sugar, packed
6 tablespoons butter
1/4 teaspoon ground cinnamon
1/3 teaspoon ground ginger

Peel carrots and cut in julienne strips, or if using baby carrots, cut in half lengthwise (makes about 3 cups). In a 2-1/2-quart covered sauce pan, cook in small amount of boiling salted water until just tender, 6 to 8 minutes. Drain into a colander.

In the same pan, mix the brown sugar, butter, cinnamon, and ginger and stir until well-blended. Add carrots and cook over low heat, stirring often, until the carrots are shiny and well glazed.

Makes 4-5 servings.

Harvard Beets

3/4 cup sugar
2 teaspoons cornstarch
1/3 cup vinegar
1/3 cup water (Use the water from the can if
  using canned beets.)
4 cups cooked, sliced beets
3 tablespoons butter
1/8 teaspoon pepper
1/4 teaspoon salt

In a 2-1/2-quart saucepan, combine the sugar and cornstarch. Add the vinegar and water and boil for 5 minutes. Add beets and simmer 1/2 hour. Add butter and season with salt and pepper.

Makes 6-8 servings.

*A*re you feeling overwhelmed and oppressed?
Try to be good to yourself.
Pray and meditate.
Take a walk.
Take a bubble bath.
Have a massage or pedicure.
Eat some comfort food.
Buy a nice CD and listen to some good music.
Take the day off and go to the lake.
Give yourself a break.

Hopping John

1 (2-ounce) envelope dry onion soup mix
2-1/2 cups water
1/4 teaspoon Tabasco sauce
1 (10-ounce) package of frozen blackeyed peas
1-1/2 cups cooked ham strips
1-1/2 cups instant rice
1-1/2 cups water

In a 2-1/2-quart saucepan, combine the onion soup mix, water, Tabasco sauce, and the peas. Cover and simmer 45 minutes. Add the ham strips and rice and the rest of the water. Bring to a boil and simmer for 5 minutes. Makes 5-6 servings.

Justus' Love Veggies

2 cloves garlic
1 medium onion, sliced
Jalapeño peppers to taste
Serrano peppers to taste
1/2 stick butter
1 cup broccoli, broken into pieces
1 zucchini squash, scrubbed and sliced thin
1 yellow summer squash, washed and sliced thin
2 cups fresh spinach, torn into pieces
2 cups shredded Jack cheese
3 to 4 cups hot, cooked rice

In a 12-inch skillet, sauté the garlic, onion, and peppers in the butter. Add the broccoli and squash and stir-fry for about 5 minutes. Top with the spinach. Top this with the cheese. Cover and simmer for about 5 minutes, or until thoroughly heated and cheese begins to melt. Serve over rice.
Makes 6-8 servings.

I believe that, when Jesus instructed us to love
our neighbor as ourselves, he meant for us to
respect and take care of ourselves just as much as
we respect and take care of others.
  Maybe he meant that we cannot love others
unless and until we love ourselves.

Sautéed Zucchini

2 tablespoons olive oil
4 zucchini, scrubbed well
Salt, pepper, and dill weed to taste

In a 12-inch skillet, heat 1 tablespoonful of the oil. Slice the zucchini into 1/4-inch slices. Cook one zucchini at a time, as that is all that will fit in the pan. Lay slices flat in the pan. Cook at medium high heat. Turn when one side gets a little brown but still crisp.

Move the slices that are in the middle of the pan to the edge as you turn them over and move those on the edges into the middle for even cooking. Sprinkle with salt, pepper, and the dill weed to taste. Add more oil and repeat for the remaining zucchini.

Makes 4-6 servings.

Spinach Stuffing

1 large onion, chopped
1 tablespoon olive oil
1 package frozen chopped spinach, thawed and
**   squeezed dry**
1 egg, lightly beaten
1 package seasoned stuffing
1/2 teaspoon garlic salt

Grease a 2-quart casserole. In a 2-1/2-quart saucepan, sauté the onion in oil. Add the remaining ingredients to the onion and pour into the casserole. Bake at 350° for 45 minutes.

Makes 4-6 servings.

*T*here is bountiful beauty, kindness, and love
in the world. All you have to do is look
around and take notice.

In your mind and in your heart, bless everyone
you meet.

Squash Elegante

3 pounds yellow or zucchini squash,
 scrubbed well and cut into thin slices
2 medium onions, sliced thin
4 ribs celery, sliced thin
1 tablespoon salt
1 (10-1/4-ounce) can cream of mushroom soup
1 pint dairy sour cream
1 (8-ounce) can sliced water chestnuts
1 (4-ounce) jar diced pimentos
2 cups shredded Cheddar cheese
1 package stove top corn bread stuffing

In a 2-1/2-quart saucepan, cook the squash, onion, and celery in salted water until the onion is clear. Drain off most of the water. Add the rest of the ingredients and mix thoroughly. Pour into a 2-quart casserole. Bake at 350° for 30 minutes.
Makes 8-10 servings.

Turnip Greens

3 strips bacon
1 (1-pound) package frozen turnip greens
1 tablespoon water
Salt to taste

Chop the bacon into very small pieces. In a slow cooker or Dutch oven, fry the bacon until brown and crisp. Add the turnips, water, and salt. Cover and cook on low for 2 hours.
Serve with hot pepper vinegar, Louisiana style.
Makes 4-6 servings.

*H*appiness is not a goal. It's a byproduct.

Vegetable Stir-Fry

1 cup onions, sliced into strips
1 cup fresh, sliced mushrooms
2 zucchini squash, scrubbed well and cut into
    4 x 1/4-inch strips
1 tablespoon olive oil
1 tablespoon water
Salt and pepper to taste.

Using a wok, cook the vegetables quickly over high heat in the oil for 5 minutes, stirring. Add the water, cover, and cook for another 2 minutes. Add seasonings.
Makes 4-6 servings.

About the Author

Peggy Grose is the mother of four and grandmother of four. She has a Master's degree in communication, is a licensed therapist, owner of her own consulting business, "Face to Face Communication," and is employed by a drug rehabilitation program. She has had extensive experience as a writer, public speaker, was once a Dale Carnegie Course instructor and sold encyclopedias, door-to-door.

Peggy admits to being a "baby freak" but loves children of all ages and is concerned with helping families become more effective. She likes swimming, writing, music, traveling, camping, dancing, and, of course, cooking.

Love and Lemon Pie

Recipes for the Body and the Soul

To order write to:

Peggy S. Grose
3801 Manchaca Road, #56 • Austin, Texas 78704

Number of copies ordered: _____ @ $18.95 = $_____

Ship to: _____

_____

_____

_____

Make checks payable to Peggy Grose. Texas residents add applicable sales tax.

Questions?

Call Peggy at (512) 444-1626
or email her at: peggy@loveandlemonpie.com.

"The quality of our relationships is directly and total determined by the quality of our communication."